2004

California Almanac & Trivia Quiz

McCormack's Guides
California 94553
ccormacks.com
ccormacks.com

Comments welcome!

Please e-mail them to bookinfo@mccormacks.com

Publisher and editor Don McCormack founded McCormack's Guides in 1984 to publish newcomer-relocation guides to California counties. A graduate of the University of California-Berkeley, McCormack worked for the Contra Costa Times, the Richmond Independent, the San Francisco Examiner and the Berkeley Gazette as a reporter, editor and columnist.

Graphics by T Graphics, Antioch, California, Cover by George Foster of Foster & Foster, Inc.

Many thanks to the people who helped make this almanac possible: Theresa Bailey, Martina Bailey, Tammy Demler, Paul Fletcher, John VanLandingham.

To Ruth — Welcome to the world!

Contents

See end of almanac for information about other books from McCormack's Guides.

For more information about McCormack's Guides, visit our web site, **www.mccormacks. com.**

California

Imagine an island ruled by fierce and fearless women, Amazons armored in gold and mounted on wild beasts, an island abundant in pearls and precious metals — an island that came to life on the pages of a 16th century Spanish novel.

Author Garcia Ordonez de Montalvo coined a new word for his fabulous island: California.

Written at the height of Spain's exploration of the New World, Montalvo's novel inspired the Spanish adventurers. When they discovered the Baja peninsula, believing it promised great riches, they called it "California."

Although California still has its El Dorado resources, its riches today lie in its climate, its people and its sense of adventure.

California compared to:

California 158,693 square miles

California

Iraq

Iraq
171,599
square miles or
about 8% bigger
than California

Japan

Italy

Italy 116,304
square miles or
73% the size of
California

Japan 143,750
square miles or
91% the size of
California

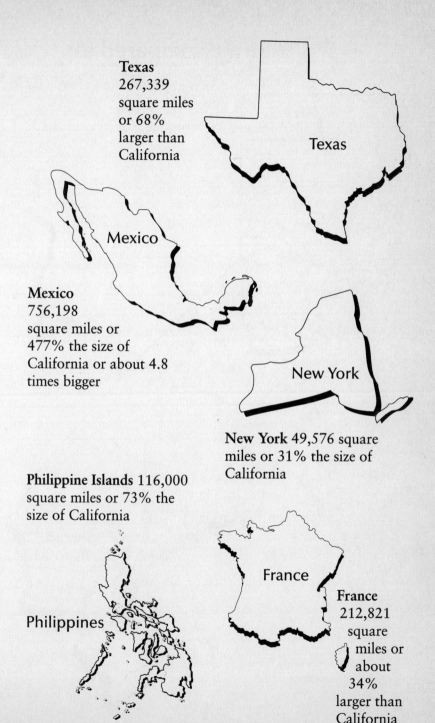

Texas 267,339 square miles or 68% larger than California

Mexico 756,198 square miles or 477% the size of California or about 4.8 times bigger

Philippine Islands 116,000 square miles or 73% the size of California

Texas

Mexico

New York

New York 49,576 square miles or 31% the size of California

Philippines

France

France 212,821 square miles or about 34% larger than California

California and Its 58 Counties

Who We Are and
Where We Live

Fastest-Growing California Cities Based on Percent

City	Population 2003	Percent Change 2002-2003
Hughson	4,920	16.0
Lincoln	20,550	15.8
Wheatland	2,690	13.5
Beaumont	13,800	13.1
Brentwood	33,000	11.5
Newport Beach	80,000	10.7
Murrieta	57,000	10.3
Soledad	24,200	10.3
Coachella	26,750	10.1
American Canyon	12,350	9.3

Q How many people have sharks attacked in California waters since 1926 when records were first kept? (Answer next page).

10 Fastest-Growing Cities Based on Numbers

City	Population 2003	Added 2002-2003
Los Angeles	3,864,400	59,000
San Diego	1,275,100	23,400
Chula Vista	199,700	9,400
Sacramento	433,400	9,000
Rancho Cucamonga	146,700	8,900
Bakersfield	266,800	8,500
San Jose	925,000	8,500
Long Beach	481,000	8,300
Irvine	164,900	7,900
Newport Beach	80,000	7,700

A Sharks have attacked 111 people since 1926 when record-keeping began. Of the eight fatalities, the last was in 1994 off the Santa Barbara Coast, says the Florida Museum of Natural History.

10 Fastest-Growing Counties Based on Percent Change

County	Population 2003	Percent Increase 2002-2003
Placer	275,600	3.7
Riverside	1,705,500	3.7
Yolo	181,300	2.8
San Joaquin	613,500	2.8
Merced	225,100	2.5
San Bernardino	1,833,000	2.5
Stanislaus	481,600	2.5
Sacramento	1,309,600	2.2
Mariposa	17,450	2.0
Lassen	34,950	2.0

10 Fastest-Growing Counties Based on Numbers

County	Population 2003	Added 2002-2003
Los Angeles	9,979,600	162,200
Riverside	1,705,500	60,200
San Diego	2,961,600	53,100
Orange	2,978,800	48,300
San Bernardino	1,833,000	44,500
Sacramento	1,309,600	28,700
San Joaquin	613,500	16,600
Fresno	841,400	14,100
Contra Costa	994,900	14,000
Kern	702,900	14,000

 In what year did California pass New York to become the most populated state in the U.S.? (Answer next page).

Population By County Historical

Counties	1950	1980	2003
Alameda	740,315	1,105,379	1,496,200
Alpine	241	1,097	1,210
Amador	9,151	19,314	36,500
Butte	64,930	143,851	210,400
Calaveras	9,902	20,710	42,450
Colusa	11,651	12,791	19,700
Contra Costa	298,984	656,380	994,900
Del Norte	8,078	18,217	27,850
El Dorado	16,207	85,812	166,000
Fresno	276,515	514,621	841,400
Glenn	15,448	21,350	27,050
Humboldt	69,241	108,514	128,300
Imperial	62,975	92,110	150,900
Inyo	11,658	17,895	18,350
Kern	228,309	403,089	702,900
Kings	46,768	73,738	136,100
Lake	11,481	36,366	61,300
Lassen	18,474	21,661	34,950
Los Angeles	4,151,687	7,477,503	9,979,600
Madera	36,964	63,116	131,200
Marin	85,619	222,568	250,400
Mariposa	5,145	11,108	17,450
Mendocino	40,854	66,738	88,200
Merced	69,780	134,560	225,100
Modoc	9,678	8,610	9,325
Mono	2,115	8,577	13,350
Monterey	130,498	290,444	415,800
Napa	46,603	99,199	129,800
Nevada	19,888	51,645	95,700
Orange	216,224	1,932,709	2,978,800
Placer	41,649	117,247	275,600
Plumas	13,519	17,340	20,900

About 1963. The exact year is a little murky since the census is taken every 10 years. The 1970 census made it official. It counted 19.9 million residents in California compared to 18.2 million residents in New York.

Population By County Historical

Counties	1950	1980	2003
Riverside	170,046	663,166	1,705,500
Sacramento	277,140	783,381	1,309,600
San Benito	14,370	25,005	56,300
San Bernardino	281,642	895,016	1,833,000
San Diego	556,808	1,861,846	2,961,600
San Francisco	775,357	678,974	791,600
San Joaquin	200,750	347,342	613,500
San Luis Obispo	51,417	155,435	256,300
San Mateo	235,659	587,329	717,000
Santa Barbara	98,220	298,694	410,300
Santa Clara	290,547	1,295,071	1,729,900
Santa Cruz	66,534	188,141	259,800
Shasta	36,413	115,715	172,000
Sierra	2,410	3,073	3,520
Siskiyou	30,733	39,732	44,400
Solano	104,833	235,203	412,000
Sonoma	103,405	299,681	472,700
Stanislaus	127,231	265,900	481,600
Sutter	26,239	52,246	83,200
Tehama	19,276	38,888	57,700
Trinity	5,087	11,858	13,300
Tulare	149,264	245,738	386,200
Tuolumne	12,584	33,928	56,500
Ventura	114,647	529,174	791,300
Yolo	40,640	113,374	181,300
Yuba	24,420	49,733	62,800
California	10,586,223	23,667,902	35,591,000

Source: California Dept. of Finance, Demographic Research Unit.

 In what era did Los Angeles pass San Francisco to become the state's most populous city: 1850-1900, 1900-1950 or 1950-2000? (Answer next page).

Native-American Place Names

Here are place names derived from Native-American languages. While most are from California tribes, a few were taken from Native-American languages of other regions.

- Awani (*Tuolumne*)—Miwok "Yosemite Valley"
- Carquinez (*Contra Costa*)—After local village
- Cotati (*Sonoma*)—After a local chief
- Cucamonga (*San Bernardino*)—Shoshone "sandy place"
- Havasu (*San Bernardino*)—Mojave "blue"
- Hetch Hetchy (*Tuolumne*)—"edible seeds or acorns"
- Inyo (*Inyo*)—Inyo for "dwelling place of a great spirit"
- Koip Peak (*Mono*)—Paiute for "mountain sheep"
- Mugu (*Ventura*)—Chumash for "beach"
- Nimshew (*Butte*) Maidu for "big water"
- Nopah Range (*Inyo*)—possibly Paiute for "no water"
- Ojai (*Ventura*)—Chumash (a'hwai) for "moon"
- Olema (*Marin*)—possibly Miwok (ole) for "coyote"
- Otay (*San Diego*)—Diegueno for "brushy"
- Paoha Island (*Mono*)—Mono for "water babies"
- Pasadena (*Los Angeles*)—Chippewa for "valley"
- Petaluma (*Sonoma*)—Miwok for "flat back"
- Pismo (*San Luis Obispo*)—probably Chumash for "tar"
- Quinado Canyon (*Monterey*)—"evil smelling"
- Requa (*Del Norte*)—Yurok (re'kwoi) for "creek mouth"
- Siskiyou (*Siskiyou*)—Cree for "bobtailed horse"
- Sisquoc (*Santa Barbara*)—possibly Chumash for "quail"
- Suisun (*Solano*)— "west winds," name of local tribe
- Temescal (*Alameda*)—Aztec for "bath house"
- Tuolumne (*Tuolumne*)—possibly Yokuts "cave people"
- Wawona (*Mariposa*)—"big tree"
- Yolla Bolly (*Trinity*)—Wintun for "snow mountain"
- Yucaipa (*San Bernardino*)—Shoshone "marshy land"
- Yuma (*Imperial*)—Yuma for "sons of the river"

 Between 1900 and 1950 San Francisco's population doubled (from 342,782 to 775,357) but during the same period the population of Los Angeles multiplied by 19 (from 102,749 to 1.97 million).

The Name's from Spain

Here are California place names of Spanish origin. See if you can match them with their English definitions. Answers on following page.

1. Alameda (*Alameda*)
2. Alamo (*Contra Costa*)
3. Alcatraz (*San Francisco*)
4. Batequitos (*San Diego*)
5. Cazadero (*Sonoma*)
6. Encinitas (*San Diego*)
7. Escondido (*San Diego*)
8. Fresno (*Fresno*)
9. Gaviota (*Santa Barbara*)
10. Hermosa (*Los Angeles*)
11. Hedionda (*Santa Clara*)
12. Pajaro (*Monterey*)
13. La Mirada (*Los Angeles*)
14. Tejon (*Kern*)
15. Las Cruces (*Santa Barbara*)
16. Sausalito (*Marin*)
17. Los Coches (*Santa Barbara*)
18. Madera (*Madera*)
19. Mariposa (*Mariposa*)
20. Palomar (*San Diego*)
21. Merced (*Merced*)
22. Nevada (*Nevada*)
23. Redondo (*Los Angeles*)
24. Rodeo (*Contra Costa*)
25. Tiburon (*Marin*)
26. Trabuco (*Orange*)

a. bird
b. butterfly
c. hunting place
d. hidden
e. seagull
f. pelican
g. wells dug in the sand
h. ash tree
i. little valley oaks
j. round
k. roundup
l. grove of poplar trees
m. wood
n. place of pigeons
o. mercy
p. cottonwood tree
q. blunderbuss
r. beautiful
s. little willow grove
t. shark
u. wild hogs
v. fetid, stinking
w. the crosses
x. the glance
y. badger
z. white as snow

 According to popular lore, how did the city of Azusa in L.A. County get its name? (Answer next page).

The Name's from Spain (answers)

1. Alameda (*Alameda*)   l. grove of poplar trees
2. Alamo (*Contra Costa*)   p. cottonwood tree
3. Alcatraz (*San Francisco*)   f. pelican
4. Batequitos (*San Diego*)   g. wells dug in the sand
5. Cazadero (Sonoma)   c. hunting place
6. Encinitas (*San Diego*)   i. little valley oaks
7. Escondido (*San Diego*)   d. hidden
8. Fresno (*Fresno*)   h. ash tree
9. Gaviota (*Santa Barbara*)   e. seagull
10. Hedionda (*Santa Clara*)   v. fetid, stinking
11. Hermosa (*Los Angeles*)   r. beautiful
12. Pajaro (Monterey)   a. bird
13. La Mirada (*Los Angeles*)   x. the glance
14. Tejon (Kern)   y. badger
15. Las Cruces (*Santa Barbara*)   w. the crosses
16. Sausalito (Marin)   s. little willow grove
17. Los Coches (*Santa Barbara*)   u. wild hogs
18. Madera (*Madera*)   m. wood
19. Mariposa (*Mariposa)*   b. butterfly
20. Palomar (San Diego))   n. place of the pigeons
21. Merced (*Merced*)   o. mercy
22. Nevada (*Nevada*)   z. white as snow
23. Redondo (*Los Angeles*)   j. round
24. Rodeo (*Contra Costa*)   k. roundup
25. Tiburon (*Marin*)   t. shark
26. Trabuco (*Orange*)   q. blunderbuss

 If we are to believe local legend, Azusa got its name because it has everything from A to Z in the USA.

Population by City

	1950	1980	2003
Alameda County			
Alameda	64,430	63,852	74,900
Albany	17,590	15,130	16,800
Berkeley	113,805	103,328	104,600
Dublin	*N.A.	13,496	35,550
Emeryville	2,889	3,714	7,550
Fremont	*N.A.	131,945	209,000
Hayward	14,272	94,167	144,700
Livermore	4,364	48,349	78,000
Newark	1,532	32,126	43,950
Oakland	384,575	339,337	412,200
Piedmont	10,132	10,498	11,150
Pleasanton	2,244	35,160	67,000
San Leandro	27,542	63,952	81,400
Union City	*N.A.	39,406	70,300
Amador County			
Amador	151	136	210
Ione	1,071	2,207	7,450
Jackson	1,879	2,331	4,060
Plymouth	382	699	1,070
Sutter Creek	1,151	1,705	2,440
Butte County			
Biggs	784	1,413	1,810
Chico	12,272	26,603	68,600
Gridley	3,054	3,982	5,750
Oroville	5,387	8,693	13,250
Paradise	*N.A.	22,571	26,700
Calaveras County			
Angels Camp	1,147	2,302	3,350

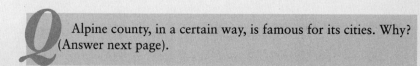

Q Alpine county, in a certain way, is famous for its cities. Why? (Answer next page).

Population by City

	1950	1980	2003
Colusa County			
Colusa	3,031	4,475	5,575
Williams	1,134	1,658	4,030
Contra Costa County			
Antioch	11,051	42,683	99,300
Brentwood	1,729	4,434	33,000
Clayton	*N.A.	4,325	11,000
Concord	6,953	103,255	124,900
Danville	*N.A.	26,446	43,200
El Cerrito	18,011	22,731	23,550
Hercules	343	5,963	20,500
Lafayette	*N.A.	20,837	24,400
Martinez	8,268	22,582	36,900
Moraga	*N.A.	15,014	16,500
Oakley	*N.A.	2,816	27,000
Orinda	*N.A.	16,825	17,850
Pinole	1,147	14,253	19,500
Pittsburg	12,763	33,034	61,100
Pleasant Hill	5,686	25,124	33,700
Richmond	99,545	74,676	101,400
San Pablo	14,476	19,750	30,750
San Ramon	*N.A.	22,356	47,050
Walnut Creek	2,420	53,643	66,000
Del Norte County			
Crescent City	1,706	3,075	7,325
El Dorado County			
Placerville	3,749	6,739	10,200
South Lake Tahoe	*N.A.	20,681	23,850

A It doesn't have any. The largest town, Markleeville, is unincorporated and the county's larger school district has only 141 students.

Population by City

	1950	1980	2003
Fresno County			
Clovis	2,766	33,021	76,000
Coalinga	5,539	6,593	16,400
Firebaugh	821	3,740	6,175
Fowler	1,857	2,496	4,270
Fresno	91,669	218,202	448,500
Huron	*N.A.	2,768	6,900
Kerman	1,563	4,002	10,000
Kingsburg	2,310	5,115	10,500
Mendota	1,516	5,038	8,175
Orange Cove	2,395	4,026	8,750
Parlier	1,419	2,902	12,150
Reedley	4,135	11,071	21,350
Sanger	6,400	12,542	19,900
San Joaquin	632	1,930	3,490
Selma	5,964	10,942	20,900
Glenn County			
Orland	2,067	4,031	6,375
Willows	3,019	4,777	6,275
Humboldt County			
Arcata	3,729	12,340	16,900
Blue Lake	824	1,201	1,160
Eureka	23,058	24,153	26,100
Ferndale	1,032	1,367	1,410
Fortuna	1,762	7,591	10,900
Rio Dell	1,862	2,687	3,180
Trinidad	188	379	310
Imperial County			
Brawley	11,922	14,946	22,550
Calexico	6,433	14,412	31,800
Calipatria	1,428	2,636	7,625

 How did the Los Angeles' town of Tarzana come by its name? (Answer next page).

Population by City

	1950	1980	2003
El Centro	12,590	23,996	38,900
Holtville	2,472	4,399	5,675
Imperial	1,759	3,451	8,450
Westmorland	1,213	1,590	2,190
Inyo County			
Bishop	2,891	*N.A.	3,620
Kern County			
Arvin	5,007	6,863	14,050
Bakersfield	34,784	105,611	266,800
California City	*N.A.	2,743	11,100
Delano	8,717	16,491	42,000
Maricopa	800	946	1,130
McFarland	2,183	5,151	10,650
Ridgecrest	2,028	15,929	25,600
Shafter	2,207	7,010	13,350
Taft	3,707	5,316	8,975
Tehachapi	1,685	4,126	11,400
Wasco	5,592	9,613	22,250
Kings County			
Avenal	3,982	4,137	15,350
Corcoran	3,150	6,454	21,150
Hanford	10,028	20,958	44,350
Lemoore	2,153	8,832	21,000
Lake County			
Clearlake	*N.A.		13,550
Lakeport	1,983	3,675	5,000
Lassen County			
Susanville	5,338	6,520	17,900

In 1919, Edgar Rice Burroughs, author of the novels about the King of the Jungle, named his estate Tarzana. The surrounding area needed a post office and a name. A contest was held and Tarzana was chosen.

Population by City

	1950	1980	2003
Los Angeles County			
Agoura Hills	*N.A.	11,399	21,950
Alhambra	51,359	64,767	88,900
Arcadia	23,066	45,993	55,500
Artesia	*N.A.	14,301	17,000
Avalon	1,506	2,022	3,320
Azusa	11,042	29,380	47,150
Baldwin Park	*N.A.	50,554	79,600
Bell	15,430	25,450	38,250
Bellflower	*N.A.	53,441	76,400
Bell Gardens	*N.A.	34,117	45,750
Beverly Hills	29,032	32,646	35,350
Bradbury	*N.A.	846	920
Burbank	78,577	84,625	104,500
Calabasas	*N.A.	*N.A.	21,100
Carson	*N.A.	81,221	94,800
Cerritos	*N.A.	53,020	54,200
Claremont	6,327	30,950	36,100
Commerce	*N.A.	10,509	13,200
Compton	47,991	81,286	97,000
Covina	3,956	32,751	48,700
Cudahy	*N.A.	17,984	25,450
Culver City	19,720	38,139	40,250
Diamond Bar	*N.A.	28,045	59,000
Downey	*N.A.	82,602	111,700
Duarte	*N.A.	16,766	22,400
El Monte	8,101	79,494	121,900
El Segundo	8,011	13,752	16,700
Gardena	14,405	45,165	60,100
Glendale	95,702	139,060	202,700
Glendora	3,988	38,654	51,500
Hawaiian Gardens	*N.A.	10,548	15,600
Hawthorne	16,316	56,447	87,400
Hermosa Beach	11,826	18,070	19,350

 Palm Springs has a pedestrian bridge over a major street near its downtown. The bridge was built not to protect pedestrians so much as motorists. Why? (Answer next page).

Population by City

	1950	1980	2003
Hidden Hills	*N.A.	1,760	2,000
Huntington Park	29,450	46,223	64,000
Industry	*N.A.	412	800
Inglewood	46,185	94,162	117,000
Irwindale	*N.A.	1,130	1,490
La Cañada Flintridge	*N.A.	20,153	21,200
La Habra Heights	*N.A.	4,786	6,075
Lakewood	*N.A.	74,654	82,300
La Mirada	*N.A.	40,986	48,900
Lancaster	3,594	48,027	126,100
La Puente	*N.A.	30,882	42,650
La Verne	4,198	23,508	32,900
Lawndale	*N.A.	23,460	32,850
Lomita	*N.A.	18,807	20,850
Long Beach	250,767	361,334	481,000
Los Angeles	1,970,358	2,966,850	3,864,400
Lynwood	25,823	48,548	72,600
Malibu	*N.A.	*N.A.	13,300
Manhattan Beach	17,330	31,542	36,300
Maywood	13,292	21,810	29,150
Monrovia	20,186	30,531	38,450
Montebello	21,735	52,929	64,700
Monterey Park	20,395	54,338	63,400
Norwalk	*N.A.	85,286	108,700
Palmdale	*N.A.	12,277	127,200
Palos Verdes Estates	1,963	14,376	13,950
Paramount	*N.A.	36,407	57,300
Pasadena	104,577	118,550	142,200
Pico Rivera	*N.A.	53,459	65,900
Pomona	35,405	92,742	156,500
Rancho Palos Verdes	*N.A.	36,577	42,800
Redondo Beach	25,226	57,102	66,500
Rolling Hills	*N.A.	2,049	1,940
Rolling Hills Estates	*N.A.	7,701	8,050

A The covered bridge connects two halves of the Desert Shadows nudist colony. Before it was built, the nudists were crossing the street and distracting the motorists.

Population by City

	1950	1980	2003
Rosemead	*N.A.	42,604	56,100
San Dimas	1,840	24,014	36,450
San Fernando	12,922	17,731	24,500
San Gabriel	20,343	30,072	41,550
San Marino	11,230	13,307	13,450
Santa Clarita	*N.A.	*N.A.	162,900
Santa Fe Springs	*N.A.	14,520	17,100
Santa Monica	71,595	88,314	89,300
Sierra Madre	7,273	10,837	10,950
Signal Hill	4,040	5,734	10,300
South El Monte	*N.A.	16,623	21,950
South Gate	51,116	66,784	100,300
South Pasadena	16,935	22,681	25,250
Temple City	*N.A.	28,972	34,700
Torrance	22,241	129,881	144,400
Vernon	432	90	95
Walnut	*N.A.	12,478	31,400
West Covina	4,499	80,291	110,500
West Hollywood	*N.A.	35,703	37,300
Westlake Village	*N.A.	6,138	8,775
Whittier	23,433	69,717	86,400
Madera County			
Chowchilla	3,893	5,122	14,350
Madera	10,497	21,732	47,000
Marin County			
Belvedere	800	2,401	2,140
Corte Madera	1,933	8,074	9,400
Fairfax	4,078	7,391	7,325
Larkspur	2,905	11,064	12,050
Mill Valley	7,331	12,967	13,650

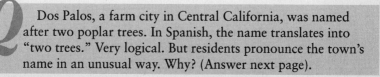

Q Dos Palos, a farm city in Central California, was named after two poplar trees. In Spanish, the name translates into "two trees." Very logical. But residents pronounce the town's name in an unusual way. Why? (Answer next page).

Population by City

	1950	1980	2003
Novato	3,496	43,916	48,650
Ross	2,179	2,801	2,350
San Anselmo	9,188	12,067	12,400
San Rafael	13,848	44,700	57,100
Sausalito	4,828	7,338	7,350
Tiburon	*N.A.	6,685	8,800
Mendocino County			
Fort Bragg	3,826	5,019	6,850
Point Arena	372	425	480
Ukiah	6,120	12,035	15,850
Willits	2,691	4,008	5,025
Merced County			
Atwater	2,856	17,530	26,000
Dos Palos	1,394	3,121	4,790
Gustine	1,984	3,142	5,125
Livingston	1,502	5,326	11,050
Los Baños	3,868	10,341	29,150
Merced	15,278	36,499	67,600
Modoc County			
Alturas	2,819	3,025	2,810
Mono County			
Mammoth Lakes	*N.A.	3,929	7,450
Monterey County			
Carmel-by-the-Sea	4,351	4,707	4,090
Del Rey Oaks	*N.A.	1,557	1,650
Gonzales	1,821	2,891	8,275
Greenfield	1,309	4,181	12,950
King City	2,347	5,495	11,300
Marina	*N.A.	20,647	19,650

Dos Palos was founded by Germans who pronounced the name, Dasche Palas. The locals still call themselves Dasche Palosians.

Population by City

	1950	1980	2003
Monterey	16,205	27,558	30,350
Pacific Grove	9,623	15,755	15,550
Salinas	13,917	80,479	150,300
Sand City	*N.A.	182	280
Seaside	10,226	36,567	33,450
Soledad	2,441	5,928	24,200
Napa County			
American Canyon	*N.A.	5,712	12,350
Calistoga	1,418	3,879	5,225
Napa	13,579	50,879	74,700
St. Helena	2,297	4,898	6,050
Yountville	*N.A.	2,893	3,280
Nevada County			
Grass Valley	5,283	6,697	12,000
Nevada City	2,505	2,431	3,030
Truckee	1,025	2,389	14,850
Orange County			
Aliso Viejo	*N.A.	*N.A.	43,900
Anaheim	14,556	219,494	337,400
Brea	3,208	27,913	37,950
Buena Park	5,483	64,165	80,600
Costa Mesa	11,844	82,562	111,500
Cypress	1,318	40,391	47,650
Dana Point	*N.A.	10,602	36,250
Fountain Valley	*N.A.	55,080	56,300
Fullerton	13,958	102,634	131,500
Garden Grove	3,762	123,307	169,900
Huntington Beach	5,237	170,505	197,000
Irvine	*N.A.	62,134	164,900
Laguna Beach	6,661	17,858	24,600
Laguna Hills	*N.A.	33,600	32,900

 With more than 20,000 square miles of area, San Bernardino, California's largest county, is larger than how many states? (Answer next page).

Population by City

	1950	1980	2003
Laguna Niguel	*N.A.	12,237	65,100
Laguna Woods	*N.A.	*N.A.	18,200
La Habra	4,961	45,232	61,200
Lake Forest	*N.A.	*N.A.	77,300
La Palma	*N.A.	15,399	15,950
Los Alamitos	*N.A.	11,529	11,800
Mission Viejo	*N.A.	50,666	98,900
Newport Beach	12,120	62,556	80,000
Orange	10,027	91,788	134,500
Placentia	1,682	35,041	49,100
Rancho Santa Margarita	*N.A.	*N.A.	48,800
San Clemente	2,008	27,325	60,700
San Juan Capistrano	*N.A.	18,959	35,200
Santa Ana	45,533	203,713	347,200
Seal Beach	3,553	25,975	24,900
Stanton	1,762	23,723	38,400
Tustin	1,143	32,317	69,800
Villa Park	*N.A.	7,137	6,200
Westminster	3,131	71,133	90,600
Yorba Linda	*N.A.	28,254	62,700
Placer County			
Auburn	4,653	7,540	12,250
Colfax	820	981	1,710
Lincoln	2,410	4,132	20,550
Loomis	*N.A.	1,284	6,175
Rocklin	1,155	7,344	43,600
Roseville	8,723	24,347	90,700
Plumas County			
Portola	2,261	1,885	2,170

Nine states are smaller than San Bernardino County: Connecticut, Delaware, Hawaii, Maryland, Massachusetts, New Hampshire, New Jersey, Rhode Island and Vermont.

Population by City

	1950	1980	2003
Riverside County			
Banning	7,034	14,020	25,500
Beaumont	3,152	6,818	13,800
Blythe	4,089	6,805	21,200
Calimesa	*N.A.	*N.A.	7,325
Canyon Lake	*N.A.	2,039	10,500
Cathedral City	*N.A.	4,130	47,300
Coachella	2,755	9,129	26,750
Corona	10,223	37,791	137,000
Desert Hot Springs	*N.A.	5,941	17,200
Hemet	3,386	22,454	62,200
Indian Wells	*N.A.	1,394	4,400
Indio	5,300	21,611	54,500
Lake Elsinore	*N.A.	5,982	33,050
La Quinta	*N.A.	3,328	30,450
Moreno Valley	*N.A.	*N.A.	150,200
Murrieta	*N.A.	*N.A.	57,000
Norco	1,584	21,126	25,250
Palm Desert	*N.A.	11,801	43,900
Palm Springs	7,660	32,271	44,000
Perris	1,807	6,827	38,200
Rancho Mirage	*N.A.	6,281	14,950
Riverside	46,764	170,876	274,100
San Jacinto	1,778	7,098	26,050
Temecula	*N.A.	1,783	75,000
Sacramento County			
Citrus Heights	*N.A.	85,911	87,200
Elk Grove	*N.A.	10,959	85,800
Folsom	1,690	11,003	63,800
Galt	1,333	5,514	22,000
Isleton	1,597	914	840
Rancho Cordova	N.A.	N.A.	**55,600
Sacramento	137,572	275,741	433,400

The names of six border towns start with "Cal" and end with fragments of next-door neighbors. Name the towns. (Answer next page).

Population by City

	1950	1980	2003
San Benito County			
Hollister	4,903	11,488	36,600
San Juan Bautista	1,031	1,276	1,610
San Bernardino County			
Adelanto	*N.A.	2,164	19,400
Apple Valley	*N.A.	14,305	58,900
Barstow	6,135	17,690	23,000
Big Bear Lake	1,434	4,896	5,875
Chino	5,784	40,165	70,700
Chino Hills	*N.A.	N.a*	73,000
Colton	14,465	21,310	50,200
Fontana	*N.A.	37,111	145,800
Grand Terrace	*N.A.	8,498	12,100
Hesperia	*N.A.	13,540	67,800
Highland	*N.A.	10,908	47,400
Loma Linda	*N.A.	10,694	20,150
Montclair	*N.A.	22,628	34,300
Needles	4,051	4,120	5,225
Ontario	22,872	88,820	165,700
Rancho Cucamonga	*N.A.	55,250	146,700
Redlands	18,429	43,619	67,600
Rialto	3,156	37,474	96,600
San Bernardino	63,058	117,490	194,100
Twentynine Palms	1,022	7,465	25,150
Upland	9,203	47,647	71,800
Victorville	3,241	14,220	72,500
Yucaipa	1,515	23,345	45,400
Yucca Valley	*N.A.	8,294	17,950
San Diego County			
Carlsbad	4,383	35,490	90,300
Chula Vista	15,927	83,927	199,700
Coronado	12,700	18,790	26,350

Calore (for Oregon), Calneva, Calvada, Calada, Calzona, Calexico.

Population by City

	1950	1980	2003
Del Mar	*N.A.	5,017	4,500
El Cajon	5,600	73,892	96,700
Encinitas	*N.A.	10,796	61,200
Escondido	6,544	64,355	138,000
Imperial Beach	*N.A.	22,689	27,600
La Mesa	10,946	50,308	55,700
Lemon Grove	*N.A.	20,780	25,350
National City	21,199	48,772	59,800
Oceanside	12,881	76,698	169,800
Poway	*N.A.	32,263	49,850
San Diego	334,387	875,538	1,275,100
San Marcos	*N.A.	17,479	63,500
Santee	*N.A.	47,080	53,600
Solana Beach	*N.A.	13,047	13,350
Vista	1,705	35,834	92,800

San Francisco County

San Francisco	775,357	678,974	791,600

San Joaquin County

Escalon	1,569	3,127	6,650
Lathrop	*N.A.	3,717	12,050
Lodi	13,798	35,221	60,500
Manteca	3,804	24,925	57,200
Ripon	1,550	3,509	11,550
Stockton	70,853	149,779	261,300
Tracy	8,410	18,428	69,600

San Luis Obispo County

Arroyo Grande	1,723	11,290	16,500
Atascadero	3,443	16,232	27,400
Grover Beach	*N.A.	8,827	13,100
Morro Bay	1,659	9,064	10,500

 Los Angeles is on the same latitude as what world capital: Lisbon, Portugal; Rabat, Morocco; or Rome, Italy? (Answer next page).

Population by City

	1950	1980	2003
Paso Robles	4,835	9,163	26,850
Pismo Beach	1,425	5,364	8,700
San Luis Obispo	14,180	34,252	44,350
San Mateo County			
Atherton	3,630	7,797	7,225
Belmont	5,567	24,505	25,400
Brisbane	*N.A.	2,969	3,650
Burlingame	19,886	26,173	28,250
Colma	297	395	1,200
Daly City	15,191	78,519	104,300
East Palo Alto	*N.A.	18,191	30,850
Foster City	*N.A.	23,287	29,850
Half Moon Bay	1,168	7,282	12,300
Hillsborough	3,552	10,451	10,950
Menlo Park	13,587	26,369	30,800
Millbrae	8,972	20,058	20,700
Pacifica	*N.A.	36,866	38,600
Portola Valley	*N.A.	3,939	4,490
Redwood City	25,544	54,951	76,000
San Bruno	12,478	35,417	40,950
San Carlos	14,371	24,710	27,750
San Mateo	41,782	77,561	93,700
So. San Francisco	19,351	49,393	60,900
Woodside	*N.A.	5,291	5,350
Santa Barbara County			
Buellton	*N.A.	2,364	4,210
Carpinteria	2,864	10,835	14,400
Guadalupe	2,429	3,629	6,275
Lompoc	5,520	26,267	41,850
Santa Barbara	44,913	74,414	90,500
Santa Maria	10,440	39,685	82,100
Solvang	*N.A.	3,091	5,450

 Rabat, Morocco.

Population by City

	1950	1980	2003
Santa Clara County			
Campbell	*N.A.	27,067	38,300
Cupertino	2,438	34,015	52,200
Gilroy	4,951	21,641	45,000
Los Altos	*N.A.	25,769	27,700
Los Altos Hills	*N.A.	7,421	8,225
Los Gatos	4,907	26,906	28,900
Milpitas	*N.A.	37,820	65,000
Monte Sereno	*N.A.	3,434	3,500
Morgan Hill	1,627	17,060	34,900
Mountain View	6,563	58,655	72,000
Palo Alto	25,475	55,225	60,500
San Jose	95,280	629,442	925,000
Santa Clara	11,702	87,746	105,800
Saratoga	1,329	29,261	30,500
Sunnyvale	9,829	106,618	132,500
Santa Cruz County			
Capitola	1,848	9,095	10,150
Santa Cruz	21,970	41,483	55,600
Scotts Valley	*N.A.	6,891	11,650
Watsonville	11,572	23,662	47,700
Shasta County			
Anderson	1,501	7,381	9,500
Redding	10,256	41,995	85,700
Shasta Lake	*N.A.	*N.A.	9,725
Sierra County			
Loyalton	911	1,030	860
Siskiyou County			
Dorris	892	836	880
Dunsmuir	2,256	2,253	1,880

What do California and Arizona share in the winter but not in the summer? (Answer next page).

Population by City

	1950	1980	2003
Etna	649	754	770
Fort Jones	525	544	660
Montague	579	1,285	1,450
Mount Shasta	1,909	2,837	3,630
Tulelake	1,028	783	1,000
Weed	2,739	2,879	2,980
Yreka	3,227	5,916	7,300
Solano County			
Benicia	7,284	15,376	27,050
Dixon	1,714	7,541	16,150
Fairfield	3,118	58,099	102,500
Rio Vista	1,831	3,142	5,725
Suisun City	946	11,087	26,850
Vacaville	3,169	43,367	93,900
Vallejo	26,038	80,303	120,100
Sonoma County			
Cloverdale	1,292	3,989	7,500
Cotati	*N.A.	3,475	6,875
Healdsburg	3,258	7,217	11,450
Petaluma	10,315	33,834	56,000
Rohnert Park	*N.A.	22,965	42,550
Santa Rosa	17,902	83,320	154,500
Sebastopol	2,601	5,595	7,800
Sonoma	2,015	6,054	9,450
Windsor	*N.A.	*N.A.	24,500
Stanislaus County			
Ceres	2,351	13,281	36,400
Hughson	1,816	2,943	4,920
Modesto	17,389	106,602	203,300
Newman	1,815	2,785	7,775
Oakdale	4,064	8,474	16,750

The same time of day. Arizona time doesn't spring forward in April or fall back in October.

Population by City

	1950	1980	2003
Patterson	1,343	3,908	13,650
Riverbank	2,662	5,695	17,250
Turlock	6,235	26,287	61,300
Waterford	1,777	2,683	7,675
Sutter County			
Live Oak	1,770	3,103	6,450
Yuba City	7,861	18,736	48,350
Tehama County			
Corning	2,537	4,745	6,825
Red Bluff	4,905	9,490	13,450
Tehama	314	365	430
Tulare County			
Dinuba	4,971	9,907	17,750
Exeter	4,078	5,606	9,600
Farmersville	*N.A.	5,544	9,250
Lindsay	5,060	6,936	10,550
Porterville	6,904	19,707	41,950
Tulare	12,445	22,526	46,250
Visalia	11,749	49,729	98,900
Woodlake	2,525	4,343	6,925
Tuolumne County			
Sonora	2,448	3,247	4,610
Ventura County			
Camarillo	*N.A.	37,797	60,500
Fillmore	3,884	9,602	14,700
Moorpark	1,146	4,030	34,550
Ojai	2,519	6,816	8,000
Oxnard	21,567	108,195	181,800
Port Hueneme	3,024	17,803	21,800

Q The first McDonald's hamburger was flipped in what town? (Answer next page).

Population by City

	1950	1980	2003
San Buenaventura	16,534	74,393	104,300
Santa Paula	11,049	20,552	28,950
Simi Valley	*N.A.	77,500	117,700
Thousand Oaks	1,243	77,072	124,000
Yolo County			
Davis	3,554	36,640	64,300
West Sacramento	*N.A.	10,875	36,550
Winters	1,265	2,652	6,600
Woodland	9,386	30,235	51,000
Yuba County			
Marysville	7,826	9,898	12,500
Wheatland	581	1,474	2,690

*N.A. Not available. In almost all cases, if not all, this indicates that the community had not yet formed itself into a legal city.
** Rancho Cordova incorporated as a legal city in 2003. The population estimate comes from census estimates.
Source: Calif. Dept. of Finance, Demographic Research Unit, which provides yearly estimates of the population of legal cities.

A Richard and Maurice McDonald, brothers from New Hampshire, opened a hot-dog stand named Airdrome in the 1930s in L.A. and later moved to San Bernardino, where they refined their methods of serving 15-cent hamburgers and 10-cent fries hot and fast. McDonald's Barbeque became the hangout place for San Berdoo teens. Ray Kroc, a salesman of milk-shake mixers, was impressed. He bought out the brothers and gave us Ronald McDonald and the Big Mac.

A Quarter of Californians Are Foreign Born

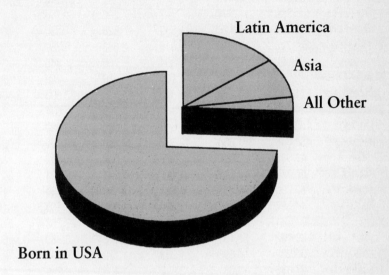

Latin America

Asia

All Other

Born in USA

One in four of California's residents— 8.9 million people — was born outside of the United States. This compares to one in ten nationally.

Almost four-fifths of foreign-born Californians live in the metropolitan areas of Los Angeles (5.1 million) or San Francisco (1.9 million).

About half of foreign-born Californians are from Latin America, while another third are from Asia. (Census 2000)

 What island is sometimes called the West's counterpart to New York's Ellis Island? (Answer next page).

Ethnic Makeup by County

County	White	Hispanic	Af.Am.	Nat. Am.	Asian	Pac. Isl.
Alameda	704,334	273,910	215,598	9,146	295,218	9,142
Alpine	890	94	7	228	4	1
Amador	30,113	3,126	1,359	626	350	36
Butte	171,728	21,339	2,816	3,866	6,752	296
Calaveras	36,982	2,765	304	705	345	38
Colusa	12,090	8,752	103	439	228	74
Contra Costa	621,490	167,776	88,813	5,830	103,993	3,466
Del Norte	21,693	3,829	1,184	1,770	637	23
El Dorado	140,209	14,566	813	1,566	3,328	209
Fresno	434,045	351,636	42,337	12,790	64,362	1,000
Glenn	18,988	7,840	155	552	893	35
Humboldt	107,179	8,210	1,111	7,241	2,091	241
Imperial	70,290	102,817	5,624	2,666	2,836	119
Inyo	14,367	2,257	29	1,802	163	15
Kern	407,581	254,036	39,798	9,999	22,268	972
Kings	69,492	56,461	10,747	2,178	3,980	250
Lake	50,289	6,639	1,233	1,772	482	93
Lassen	27,336	4,681	2,992	1,104	249	146
Los Angeles	4,637,062	4,242,213	930,957	76,988	1,137,500	27,053
Madera	76,612	54,515	5,072	3,212	1,566	210
Marin	207,800	27,351	7,142	1,061	11,203	388
Mariposa	15,234	1,329	114	602	122	22
Mendocino	69,671	14,213	536	4,103	1,038	126
Merced	118,350	95,466	8,064	2,510	14,321	396
Modoc	8,120	1,088	65	398	58	7
Mono	10,818	2,274	61	309	143	11
Monterey	224,682	187,969	15,050	4,202	24,245	1,789
Napa	99,396	29,416	1,645	1,045	3,694	289

A Angel Island in San Francisco Bay. In 1882, following an economic downturn and agitation over immigration that might drive down wages, the U.S. passed laws barring Chinese immigrants. Prejudice was also at work. But the laws allowed immigration of Chinese nationals who were related to U.S. citizens. Over 30 years, the Angel Island Immigration Station, opened in 1910, was the point of entry for about 175,000 Chinese immigrants. The station was abandoned in 1940, after a fire.

Ethnic Makeup by County

County	White	Hispanic	Af.Am.	Nat. Am.	Asian	*Pac. Is.
Nevada	85,948	5,201	259	814	715	81
Orange	1,844,652	875,579	47,649	19,906	386,785	8,938
Placer	220,053	24,019	2,031	2,199	7,317	386
Plumas	19,113	1,177	130	530	110	20
Riverside	1,013,478	559,575	96,421	18,168	56,954	3,902
Sacramento	783,240	195,890	121,804	13,359	134,899	7,264
San Benito	34,695	25,516	573	616	1,277	99
San Bernardino	1,060,960	669,387	155,348	19,915	80,217	5,110
San Diego	1,871,839	750,965	161,480	24,337	249,802	13,561
San Francisco	385,728	109,504	60,515	3,458	239,565	3,844
San Joaquin	327,607	172,073	37,689	6,377	64,283	1,955
San Luis Obispo	208,699	40,196	5,002	2,335	6,568	286
San Mateo	420,683	154,708	24,840	3,140	141,684	9,403
Santa Barbara	290,418	136,668	9,195	4,784	16,344	700
Santa Clara	905,660	403,401	47,182	11,350	430,095	5,773
Santa Cruz	191,931	68,486	2,477	2,461	8,789	382
Shasta	145,826	8,998	1,225	4,528	3,048	178
Sierra	3,348	213	7	67	6	3
Siskiyou	38,573	3,354	580	1,726	526	57
Solano	222,387	69,598	58,827	3,110	50,299	3,078
Sonoma	374,209	79,511	6,522	5,389	14,098	934
Stanislaus	309,901	141,871	11,521	5,676	18,848	1,529
Sutter	53,291	17,529	1,509	1,225	8,884	161
Tehama	47,518	8,871	318	1,178	440	55
Trinity	11,573	517	58	631	61	15
Tulare	213,751	186,846	5,852	5,737	12,018	408
Tuolumne	48,750	4,445	1,146	992	395	91
Ventura	526,721	251,734	14,664	7,106	40,284	1,671
Yolo	114,129	43,707	3,425	1,953	16,614	507
Yuba	42,537	10,449	1,904	1,569	4,519	123

*Pac. Is. includes native Hawaiians.

Source: Census 2000

 What major California City was established by a settlement party composed mainly of Native Hawaiians? (Answer next page).

U.S. Population By State

States	Population	States	Population
Alabama	4,486,508	New Mexico	1,855,059
Alaska	643,786	New York	19,157,532
Arizona	5,456,453	North Carolina	8,320,146
Arkansas	2,710,079	North Dakota	634,110
California	35,116,033	Ohio	11,421,267
Colorado	4,506,542	Oklahoma	3,493,714
Connecticut	3,460,503	Oregon	3,521,515
Delaware	807,385	Pennsylvania	12,335,091
Florida	16,713,149	Rhode Island	1,069,725
Georgia	8,560,310	South Carolina	4,107,183
Hawaii	1,244,898	South Dakota	761,063
Idaho	1,341,131	Tennessee	5,797,289
Illinois	12,600,620	Texas	21,779,893
Indiana	6,159,068	Utah	2,316,256
Iowa	2,936,760	Vermont	616,592
Kansas	2,715,884	Virginia	7,293,542
Kentucky	4,092,891	Washington	6,068,996
Louisiana	4,482,646	West Virginia	1,801,873
Maine	1,294,464	Wisconsin	5,441,196
Maryland	5,458,137	Wyoming	498,703
Massachusetts	6,427,801	Washington D.C.	570,898
Michigan	10,050,446	U.S.	288,368,698
Minnesota	5,019,720		
Mississippi	2,871,782		
Missouri	5,672,579		
Montana	909,453		
Nebraska	1,729,180		
Nevada	2,173,491		
New Hampshire	1,275,056		
New Jersey	8,590,300		

Source: 2002, U.S. Census bureau. Numbers differ from other charts because California also does informal updates annually and we favor the California estimates over the U.S. Census data, which comes out every two years or so. Because we are using U.S. Census data in this chart for all the other states, however, we decided not to mix in numbers from California sources.

 Sacramento was established by John Sutter who entered California after visiting the Sandwich {Hawaiian} Islands where he recruited native workers.

Where Immigrants Hail From
Legal Immigration to U.S.

Afghanistan	463	Canada	3,509
Albania	51	Cape Verde	2
Algeria	138	Cayman Islands	1
American Samoa	8	Chad	2
Andorra	1	Chile	377
Angola	7	China, People's Republic	17,312
Antigua-Barbuda	7	Columbia	1,162
Argentina	752	Congo, Democratic	22
Armenia	1,390	Congo, Republic of	37
Aruba	4	Cook Islands	3
Australia	647	Costa Rica	272
Austria	82	Cote D'Ivoire	33
Azerbaijan	257	Croatia	205
Bahamas	18	Cuba	546
Bahrain	21	Cyprus	38
Bangladesh	661	Czech Republic	68
Barbados	15	Czechoslovakia, former	178
Belarus	480	Denmark	189
Belgium	155	Djibouti	3
Belize	412	Dominican Republic	82
Benin	8	Ecuador	615
Bermuda	9	Egypt	793
Bhutan	1	El Salvador	11,929
Bolivia	202	Eritrea	131
Bosnia-Herzegovina	1,058	Estonia	51
Botswana	1	Ethiopia	764
Brazil	1,332	Fiji	1,141
British Virgin Islands	1	Finland	112
Brunei	3	France	1,423
Bulgaria	607	French Guiana	1
Burkina Faso	5	French Polynesia	5
Burma	709	Gabon	3
Burundi	2	Gambia	11
Cambodia	796	Georgia	186
Cameroon	66	Germany	1,944

 In 1812, the Russians established a coastal fort in Northern California that came to be known as Fort Ross. Who was Ross? (Answer next page).

Where Immigrants Hail From
Legal Immigration to U.S.

Ghana	189	Lithuania	171
Gibraltar	1	Luxembourg	9
Greece	166	Macau	173
Grenada	8	Macedonia	29
Guadeloupe	2	Madagascar	12
Guatemala	6,009	Malawi	11
Guinea	1	Malaysia	760
Guinea-Bissau	9	Mali	6
Guyana	100	Malta	6
Haiti	77	Marshall Islands	1
Honduras	1,213	Mauritania	11
Hong Kong	3,851	Mauritius	10
Hungary	299	Mexico	97,151
Iceland	26	Moldova	572
India	16,512	Monaco	3
Indonesia	1,205	Mongolia	23
Iran	4,900	Montserrat	5
Iraq	802	Morocco	291
Ireland	325	Mozambique	10
Israel	1,063	Namibia	7
Italy	651	Nepal	120
Jamaica	299	Netherlands	361
Japan	3,632	Netherlands Antilles	7
Jordan	826	New Caledonia	1
Kazakhstan	306	New Zealand	338
Kenya	267	Nicaragua	5,076
Korea	7,235	Niger	418
Kuwait	231	Nigeria	517
Kyrgyzstan	61	Northern Mariana Islands	1
Laos	387	Norway	117
Latvia	122	Oman	4
Lebanon	1,085	Pakistan	2,387
Liberia	82	Palau	1
Libya	43	Panama	221
Liechtenstein	1	Papua New Guinea	4

A Nobody. The name was derived from Rossiya, the name for Russia in Tsarist days. The fort was established to supply Russian outposts in Alaska and to trap otter. The venture never made money and in 1841 the Russians just sailed away.

Where Immigrants Hail From
Legal Immigration to U.S.

Paraguay	30	Swaziland	1
Peru	2,016	Sweden	432
Philippines	23,176	Switzerland	397
Poland	445	Syria	893
Portugal	137	Taiwan	6,768
Puerto Rico	1	Tajikistan	17
Qatar	18	Tanzania	76
Romania	986	Thailand	1,540
Russia	3,472	Togo	8
Rwanda	4	Tonga	155
Samoa	45	Trinidad & Tobago	158
Saudi Arabia	190	Tunisia	67
Senegal	50	Turkey	568
Seychelles	3	Turkmenistan	20
Sierra Leone	98	Uganda	67
Singapore	445	Ukraine	3,948
Slovak Republic	83	United Arab Emirates	67
Slovenia	17	United Kingdom	4,076
Solomon Islands	1	Uruguay	51
Somalia	85	Uzbekistan	311
South Africa	824	Vanuatu	1
Soviet Union, Former	342	Venezuela	354
Spain	347	Vietnam	13,025
Sri Lanka	462	Western Sahara	1
St. Kitts-Nevis	5	Yemen	310
St. Lucia	17	Yugoslavia, Former	462
St. Vincent & Grenadines	17	Zambia	41
Sudan	91	Zimbabwe	65
Suriname	9		

Source: Legal Immigration to California 2001. Cal. Dept. of Finance, Demographic Research Unit

 San Francisco State University President S. I. Hayakawa held what distinction as a politician? (Answer next page).

Top 30 Baby Names California

Boys		Girls	
Daniel	4,099	Emily	3,012
Anthony	3,753	Ashley	2,667
Jose	3,533	Samantha	2,534
Andrew	3,521	Jessica	1,991
Jacob	3,351	Jennifer	1,976
Joshua	3,343	Isabella	1,875
Michael	3,205	Alyssa	1,870
David	3,162	Elizabeth	1,696
Matthew	3,080	Jasmine	1,657
Angel	2,907	Natalie	1,633
Christopher	2,884	Alexis	1,577
Jonathan	2,714	Sarah	1,548
Joseph	2,674	Madison	1,525
Alexander	2,377	Hannah	1,486
Kevin	2,339	Stephanie	1,463
Ryan	2,279	Brianna	1,457
Christian	2,253	Andrea	1,338
Brandon	2,251	Sophia	1,321
Ethan	2,249	Maria	1,301
Nicholas	2,190	Emma	1,285
Juan	2,042	Michelle	1,276
Luis	1,970	Vanessa	1,253
Jesus	1,969	Victoria	1,208
Nathan	1,934	Kimberly	1,207
Justin	1,926	Leslie	1,206
Gabriel	1,783	Lauren	1,204
Carlos	1,767	Kayla	1,184
Adrian	1,671	Abigail	1,177
Bryan	1,652	Olivia	1,088
Jason	1,595	Mia	1,080

Source: California Dept. of Health Services, 2002 births

A Known to his campus colleagues as "Don," Hayakawa was the first Japanese-American elected to the U.S. Senate after his popular handling of student unrest in the 1960s and 1970s.

2

Geography & Environment

In forests, lakes, beaches, mountains and places to explore and play, California is truly blessed.

In some regions it is possible to hike in the desert, ski on a mountain, and surf a Pacific wave, all in the same day.

Only in recent decades have many Californians been truly aware of the need to protect and restore nature's gifts.

Much progress has been made. Water quality in bays and rivers and in discharges to the ocean has been greatly improved.

In the 1950s and 1960s, many cities, especially in Southern California, were afflicted with heavy smogs, generated by emissions from cars and industries. Thanks to changes in design and tougher laws, California is enjoying some of its cleanest air in decades.

Many problems remain. With the coastal cities filling with people, many residents have moved to inland counties and cities creating long commutes and taking over land that was once used for farming. Smog now is a problem in some inland regions. The state recently passed laws that will cut auto emissions even more. Planning and preserving open space have become top priorities in many areas.

For the future, many argue that if California is to save its natural treasures, it will have to do a much better job of managing growth. California — a great place to live but if it is to stay great, we have to treat it wiser and kindlier.

 The world's tallest tree is located in California. What is its name and how tall is it? (Answer next page).

Emblems of California

Flower — California Poppy

Artifact — Native-American chipped-stone bear

Insect — California Dog-face Butterfly

Bird — California Quail

Fossil — Saber-Toothed Cat

Animal — Grizzly Bear

 The world's tallest tree is a 367.5-footer, unofficially known as the "Mendocino Tree." It stands in the Montgomery Woods State Reserve near Ukiah among a grove of about 24 redwoods, all of which tower over 350 feet.

Marine Mammal — Gray Whale

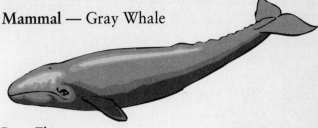

Flag — Bear Flag

Gemstone — Benitoite

Tree — Redwood

Mineral — Gold

Rock — Serpentine

 **Fish** — Golden Trout

Colors — Blue and Gold

Motto — Eureka *"I have found it"*

Reptile — Desert Tortoise

 Where in California did the saber-toothed cat roam? (Answer next page).

Lake Tahoe

Tenth-deepest lake in the world and second-deepest in United States. Lake Tahoe was formed over 1 million years ago after glaciers gouged out what is now known as the Tahoe basin. Its maximum depth was measured at 1,645 feet, second only to Oregon's Crater Lake, 1,949 feet.

Highest lake of its size in the U.S. — elevation 6,225 feet above sea level.

Name comes from a Washoe Indian word "da'au," or lake, which evolved into Tahoe. Other early names were Mountain Lake, Lake Bonpland and Lake Bigler, for an early governor. Union sympathizers during Civil War promoted Tahoe in retaliation for the governor's southern sympathies. In 1945, state legislature made Lake Tahoe the official name.

Drain Lake Tahoe you have enough water to supply every man, woman and child in the U.S. with 50 gallons daily for five years or enough cover a flat surface the size of California to a depth of 14 inches. If the City of Los Angeles could find a way to capture and transport just the water evaporating from the

The saber-toothed cat roamed the hills in and around Hollywood. Many ended up in the tar pits in West L.A., now the site of the Page Museum.

lake in one year, it would have enough to satisfy its needs for about five years.

Clear and cold. Surface temperature ranges between 40 and 50 degrees in February and March and between 65 to 70 during August and September, cooler even in summer than your bathtub. Yet, because of the continuous movement of water, Lake Tahoe never freezes.

Lake Tahoe measures 12 miles wide and 22 miles long and has a shoreline of 72 miles.

Movie buffs will remember that scenes from "The Godfather," Parts I and II, were shot at Lake Tahoe. The lake also has appeared in several other Hollywood productions including "Rainman," "Rose Marie" and the television series "Bonanza." It even doubled as Scotland's Loch Ness for a thriller called "The Loch Ness Horror."

Recreation paradise: downhill and cross-country skiing, boating, gambling, fishing, hunting, golfing, camping and bicycling. The Lake Tahoe area has the best ski resorts in the state and one, Squaw Valley, hosted the 1960s winter Olympics.

Lake Tahoe straddles the border of California and Nevada; gambling casinos on the Nevada side. Efforts are underway to curtail pollution in the lake and keep it crystal clear.

 In what month do the swallows return to the mission at Capistrano? When do they leave? (Answer next page).

California Rivers Over 50 Miles in Length

River	Miles	River	Miles
Amargosa	140	Owens	125
American	60	Pajaro	100
Bear	60	Russian	100
Calaveras	72	Sacramento	373
Carson	160	Salinas	179
Chowchilla	78	San Antonio	59
Colorado	1,450	San Benito	100
Cosumnes	102	San Gabriel	65
Eel	197	San Joaquin	370
Feather	80	San Luis Rey	54
Fresno	87	Santa Ana	100
Kern	164	Santa Clara	75
Kings	176	Santa Margarita	60
Klamath	180	Scott	68
Mad	90	Stanislaus	148
Mattole	65	Trinity	128
Merced	150	Truckee	110
McCloud	60	Tule	91
Mojave	100	Tuolumne	162
Mokelumne	140	Van Duzen	75
Nacimiento	65	Walker	186
Napa	53	Yuba	70
Navarro	56		

Major California Waterfalls

Waterfall	Location	Feet
Ribon	Yosemite National Park	1,612
Upper Yosemite	Yosemite National Park	1,430
Silver Strand	Yosemite National Park	1,170
Middle Cascade	Yosemite National Park	909
Feather	Plumas National Park	640
Bridalveil	Yosemite National Park	620
Nevada	Yosemite National Park	594
Illilouette	Yosemite National Park	370
Lower Yosemite	Yosemite National Park	320
Vernal	Yosemite National Park	317

 Fifties crooner Pat Boone warbled "When the swallows come back to Capistrano" but never revealed the "when." For the record, says the local chamber of commerce, they arrive early in March and leave around the second week of October.

Major California Earthquakes Since 1872

Date	Location	Richter
March 26, 1872	Owens Valley	7.8
November 23, 1873	Del Norte County	6.7
January 24, 1875	Lassen and Plumas Counties	5.8
February 2, 1881	Monterey	5.6
April 10, 1881	Stanislaus County	5.9
May 19, 1889	Contra Costa County	6
February 24, 1892	San Diego County	6.7
April 19, 1892	Solano County	6.4
June 20, 1897	Santa Clara County	6.2
March 31, 1898	San Pablo Bay	6.2
April 15, 1898	Mendocino County	6.4
April 19, 1898	Solano and Yolo Counties	6.4
December 25, 1899	Riverside County	6.6
April 18, 1906	San Francisco	8.3
July 29, 1925	Santa Barbara	6.3
March 10, 1933	Long Beach	6.3
May 18, 1940	Imperial Valley	7.1
June 30, 1941	Santa Barbara	5.9
July 21, 1952	Kern County	7.7
December 21, 1954	Eureka	6.6
February 9, 1971	San Fernando	6.4
October 15, 1979	Imperial Valley	6.6
May 2, 1983	Coalinga (Fresno County)	6.7
April 24, 1984	Morgan Hill	6.2
November 23, 1984	near Bishop	6.1
July 21, 1986	Chalfant Valley (Near Bishop)	6.5
October 1, 1987	Whittier-Narrows	5.9
November 24, 1987	Superstition Hills (Imperial City)	6
October 17, 1989	Loma Prieta	7.1
April 25, 1992	Petrolia (Humboldt County)	7.2
June 28, 1992	Big Bear area (San Bernardino Co.)	6.7–7.6
January 17, 1994	Northridge (Los Angeles)	6.7
October 16, 1999	Bullion Mountains (San Bernardino Co.)	7.4

 When and where in California did the last volcano blow its lid? (Answer next page).

Highest Points in Each County

County	Highest Point	Elevation Feet
Alameda	Discovery Peak	3,840
Alpine	Sonora Peak	11,459
Amador	Thunder Mountain	9,410
Butte	Lost Lake Ridge	7,120
Calaveras	Corral Ridge	8,170
Colusa	Snow Mountain East	7,040
Contra Costa	Mt. Diablo	3,849
Del Norte	Bear Mountain	6,400
El Dorado	Freel Peak	10,881
Fresno	North Palisade	14,242
Glenn	Black Butte	7,448
Humboldt	Salmon Mountain	6,956
Imperial	Blue Angels Peak	4,548
Inyo*	Mt. Whitney	14,491
Kern	Saw Mill Mountain	8,818
Kings	Table Mountain	3,473
Lake	Snow Mountain East	7,056
Lassen	Hat Mountain	8,737
Los Angeles	Mt. San Antonio	10,064
Madera	Mt. Ritter	13,143
Marin	Mt. Tamalpais	2,571
Mariposa	Parsons Peak Ridge	12,040
Mendocino	Anthony Peak	6,954
Merced	Laveaga Peak	3,801
Modoc	Eagle Peak	9,892
Mono	White Mountain Peak	14,246
Monterey	Junipero Serra Peak	5,862
Napa	Mt. Saint Helena	4,200
Nevada	Mt. Lola	9,148

 On May 22, 1915, Mt. Lassen, located east of Redding, culminated a year of 107 eruptions by exploding. The explosion flattened trees up to a mile away.

Elevations by County

County	Highest Point	Elevation
Orange	Santiago Peak	5,687
Placer	Granite Chief	9,006
Plumas	Mt. Ingalls	8,372
Riverside	San Jacinto Peak	10,804
Sacramento	Carpenter Hill	828
San Benito	San Benito Mountain	5,241
San Bernardino	San Gorgonio Mountain	11,502
San Diego	Hot Springs Mountain	6,533
San Francisco	Mt. Davidson	927
San Joaquin	Mt. Boardman North	3,626
San Luis Obispo	Caliente Mountain	5,106
San Mateo	Long Ridge	2,600
Santa Barbara	Big Pine Mountain	6,800
Santa Clara	Copernicus Peak	4,360
Santa Cruz	Mt. McPherson	3,231
Shasta	Lassen Peak	10,457
Sierra	Mt. Lola North	8,844
Siskiyou	Mt. Shasta	14,162
Solano	Mt. Vaca	2,819
Sonoma	Cobb Mountain West Rim	4,480
Stanislaus	Mt. Stakes	3,804
Sutter	South Butte	2,120
Tehoma	Brokeoff Mountain	9,235
Trinity	Mt. Eddy	9,025
Tulare*	Mt. Whitney	14,491
Tuolumne	Mt. Lyell	13,114
Ventura	Mt. Pinos	8,831
Yolo	Little Blue Peak	3,120
Yuba	Sugar Pine Peak	4,825

* Mt. Whitney straddles Tulare and Inyo counties.

 Mt. Whitney (14,491 ft.), is the highest mountain in the continental U.S. Name the highest mountain in the entire U.S. and its approximate height. (Answer next page).

Land and Water Areas of Counties

County	Water Sq. Mi.	Land Sq. Mi.	Total Sq.Mi.
Alameda	84	738	821
Alpine	5	739	743
Amador	12	593	605
Butte	38	1,640	1,677
Calaveras	17	1,020	1,037
Colusa	6	1,151	1,156
Contra Costa	82	720	802
Del Norte	222	1,008	1,230
El Dorado	77	1,711	1,788
Fresno	55	5,963	6,017
Glenn	12	1,315	1,327
Humboldt	480	3,573	4,052
Imperial	307	4,175	4,482
Inyo	24	10,203	10,227
Kern	21	8,141	8,162
Kings	1	1,391	1,392
Lake	72	1,258	1,330
Lassen	163	4,557	4,720
Los Angeles	692	4,061	4,752
Madera	18	2,136	2,153
Marin	308	520	828
Mariposa	12	1,451	1,463
Mendocino	369	3,509	3,878
Merced	43	1,929	1,972
Modoc	259	3,944	4,203
Mono	87	3,044	3,132
Monterey	449	3,322	3,771
Napa	35	754	788
Nevada	17	958	975
Orange	159	789	948
Placer	98	1,404	1,503

The highest mountain in the U.S. is Mt. McKinley, 20,320 ft., located in Alaska. Many climbers refer to it by its Native-American name, Denali, meaning "great one."

Land and Water Areas of Counties

County	Water Sq. Mi.	Land Sq. Mi.	Total Sq.Mi.
Plumas	60	2,554	2,614
Riverside	96	7,207	7,303
Sacramento	30	966	996
San Benito	2	1,389	1,391
San Bernardino	53	20,053	20,105
San Diego	326	4,200	4,526
San Francisco	185	47	232
San Joaquin	27	1,399	1,426
San Luis Obispo	311	3,304	3,616
San Mateo	292	449	741
Santa Barbara	1,052	2,737	3,789
Santa Clara	13	1,291	1,304
Santa Cruz	162	445	607
Shasta	62	3,785	3,847
Sierra	9	953	962
Siskiyou	61	6,287	6,348
Solano	78	829	907
Sonoma	192	1,576	1,768
Stanislaus	21	1,494	1,515
Sutter	6	603	609
Tehama	11	2,951	2,962
Trinity	29	3,179	3,208
Tulare	15	4,824	4,839
Tuolumne	39	2,235	2,274
Ventura	363	1,845	2,208
Yolo	10	1,013	1,023
Yuba	13	631	644
California*	7,736	155,959	163,696

*Other Total: See Trivia Question below.
Source: California Dept. of Water Resources.

 The state puts the total area of California at 163,696 sq. miles. On page 6, we state the area of California is 158,693 sq. miles. Why the difference? (Answer next page).

Average Temperatures

City	Jan	Mar	May	Jul	Aug	Sep	Nv	Yr. Avg.
Anaheim	58	60	66	74	76	74	63	66
Auburn	45	51	63	77	76	72	53	60
Bakersfield	46	58	70	85	83	75	55	65
Barstow	48	57	70	84	84	77	55	65
Big Bear Lake	34	37	50	64	63	57	40	47
Borrego Springs	56	64	77	91	91	85	64	73
Chula Vista	55	57	62	68	70	69	59	62
Culver City	56	58	63	70	71	70	61	63
Death Valley	52	67	85	101	99	90	62	76
Escondido	56	59	66	75	76	74	60	65
Eureka	48	49	53	57	58	57	52	53
Folsom	44	52	65	77	75	73	55	61
Gilroy	48	55	63	71	71	69	54	60
Half Moon Bay	51	52	54	58	59	59	54	55
Laguna Beach	54	56	62	68	69	68	59	61
Long Beach	57	59	65	73	75	73	61	65
Los Ang. Dwntn	57	60	65	73	74	72	63	65
Modesto	46	55	66	77	75	72	53	61
Oakland	49	54	59	64	64	65	55	58
Palmdale	45	53	66	81	80	74	53	62
Palm Springs	56	64	77	91	90	85	64	73
Pasadena	55	58	65	74	75	73	61	64
Redding	46	53	67	79	77	72	50	61
Riverside	53	57	66	77	77	74	59	64
San Diego	56	59	63	70	71	70	61	63
San Rafael	49	55	61	68	68	67	56	59
Santa Barbara	54	57	61	67	68	67	59	61
Stockton	45	54	66	77	76	73	53	61
Thermal	55	64	78	91	90	85	62	72
Tustin	54	57	64	72	72	71	59	63
Walnut Creek	45	52	61	71	70	68	53	58
Yorba Linda	54	57	64	74	74	72	60	64

Source: Western Regional Climate Center

 Many reference guides do not credit coastal waters to a state's area. The California government does, greatly increasing the size of some counties. See San Francisco.

Average Minimum Temperatures

City	Jan	Mar	May	Jul	Aug	Sep	Nv	Yr. Avg.
Anaheim	47	50	57	63	64	62	51	55
Auburn	36	41	50	62	61	57	42	48
Bakersfield	35	44	56	68	66	58	40	50
Barstow	31	39	53	67	65	58	37	48
Big Bear Lake	20	24	34	47	46	40	25	32
Borrego Springs	37	45	56	70	70	63	44	53
Chula Vista	45	49	56	64	65	63	50	54
Culver City	45	48	54	61	62	60	50	53
Death Valley	39	54	71	87	85	75	48	62
Escondido	38	42	51	59	60	57	42	48
Eureka	42	43	48	52	53	52	45	47
Folsom	35	40	50	59	57	56	43	47
Gilroy	37	42	48	54	54	52	41	46
Half Moon Bay	43	44	47	52	53	52	46	47
Laguna Beach	43	46	53	59	60	58	47	51
Long Beach	46	49	55	62	63	61	51	54
Los Ang. Dwntn	48	51	57	63	64	63	53	56
Modesto	38	43	52	60	59	56	42	48
Oakland	39	43	49	53	53	54	46	47
Palmdale	32	39	50	65	64	57	38	47
Palm Springs	42	48	60	75	74	68	49	57
Pasadena	43	46	53	60	61	59	47	51
Redding	37	43	55	68	66	61	44	52
Riverside	40	43	52	60	60	57	43	49
San Diego	48	52	58	64	66	64	53	56
San Rafael	41	45	49	54	54	54	46	48
Santa Barbara	42	46	52	57	58	57	47	50
Stockton	38	43	52	61	60	57	42	49
Thermal	39	48	63	76	75	67	45	56
Tustin	40	44	52	59	59	57	44	50
Walnut Creek	35	39	46	53	53	51	40	44
Yorba Linda	42	44	51	58	59	57	46	49

Source: Western Regional Climate Center

How wide is the wingspan of a California Condor?
(Answer next page).

Average Maximum Temperatures

City	Jan	Mar	May	Jul	Aug	Sep	Nov	Yr. Avg.
Anaheim	69	71	76	84	87	85	75	77
Auburn	54	62	76	93	91	86	63	72
Bakersfield	56	71	85	102	101	92	70	79
Barstow	60	70	86	102	100	94	69	80
Big Bear Lake	47	51	66	80	79	74	54	62
Borrego Springs	68	77	91	106	104	101	78	87
Chula Vista	65	65	68	73	75	75	69	69
Culver City	67	68	72	78	79	79	72	73
Death Valley	66	81	99	115	114	106	76	91
Escondido	69	70	77	87	89	87	74	77
Eureka	54	55	58	62	63	63	58	58
Folsom	52	63	80	96	94	90	66	74
Gilroy	60	67	78	88	88	86	67	74
Half Moon Bay	58	60	61	64	65	67	63	62
Laguna Beach	65	67	71	76	78	77	70	71
Long Beach	67	68	74	83	84	82	72	74
Los Ang. Dwntn	66	69	73	82	83	82	73	74
Modesto	54	67	81	94	92	88	64	75
Oakland	55	61	67	71	71	74	63	65
Palmdale	58	67	81	97	97	91	67	77
Palm Springs	69	79	94	108	107	102	79	89
Pasadena	67	70	77	89	90	87	74	77
Redding	57	64	83	97	96	89	62	76
Riverside	66	70	79	94	94	90	73	79
San Diego	65	66	69	75	76	76	70	70
San Rafael	56	65	73	82	82	81	65	70
Santa Barbara	65	67	70	76	78	77	71	71
Stockton	53	66	81	94	93	88	64	74
Thermal	71	80	94	107	105	101	79	88
Tustin	67	69	75	84	86	85	74	76
Walnut Creek	55	65	76	88	87	85	66	72
Yorba Linda	67	70	77	89	89	87	74	78

Source: Western Regional Climate Center

An adult California Condor weighs about 20 pounds and has a wingspan of about 9 feet.

Average Days Below 32F

City	Jan	Feb	Mar	Apr	Oct	Nov	Dec	Yr. Avg.
Anaheim	0	0	0	0	0	0	0	0
Auburn	9	3	2	0	0	1	8	23
Bakersfield	11	3	0	0	0	3	11	28
Barstow	18	10	4	0	0	8	19	60
Big Bear Lake	29	26	29	24	17	26	29	200
Borrego Springs	8	4	1	0	0	2	6	20
Chula Vista	0	0	0	0	0	0	0	1
Culver City	0	0	0	0	0	0	0	0
Death Valley	4	1	0	0	0	0	6	12
Escondido	8	4	1	0	0	2	6	22
Eureka	2	1	0	0	0	0	2	5
Folsom	11	5	2	0	0	2	8	29
Gilroy	10	4	1	0	0	3	10	27
Half Moon Bay	1	0	0	0	0	0	0	1
Laguna Beach	1	0	0	0	0	0	1	3
Long Beach	0	0	0	0	0	0	0	0
Los Ang. Dwntn	0	0	0	0	0	0	0	0
Modesto	7	3	1	0	0	2	7	20
Oakland	4	1	0	0	0	0	2	8
Palmdale	17	10	5	1	0	7	16	57
Palm Springs	3	1	0	0	0	0	2	6
Pasadena	1	0	0	0	0	0	0	2
Redding	8	2	2	0	0	1	5	18
Riverside	5	3	1	0	0	1	4	14
San Diego	0	0	0	0	0	0	0	0
San Rafael	2	0	0	0	0	0	1	4
Santa Barbara	1	1	0	0	0	0	0	2
Stockton	10	4	1	0	0	3	9	27
Thermal	6	2	0	0	0	1	6	16
Tustin	3	2	1	0	0	1	2	9
Walnut Creek	14	8	4	1	0	5	11	43
Yorba Linda	2	1	0	0	0	0	2	6

Source: Western Regional Climate Center. Note: Very few summer days go below 32F.

What percentage of California qualifies as desert: 4 or 14 or 24 percent? (Answer next page).

Average Days Above 90F

City	Apr	May	Jun	Jul	Aug	Sep	Oct	Yr. Avg.
Anaheim	1	1	3	4	10	10	4	33
Auburn	0	3	10	21	20	11	2	68
Bakersfield	2	11	19	30	30	18	7	117
Barstow	3	12	24	31	30	23	7	129
Big Bear Lake	0	0	0	1	0	0	0	1
Borrego Springs	11	19	27	31	30	28	19	168
Chula Vista	0	0	0	0	0	1	0	2
Culver City	0	0	0	0	1	2	2	7
Death Valley	16	26	29	31	31	29	21	189
Escondido	1	2	4	10	13	10	4	46
Eureka	0	0	0	0	0	0	0	0
Folsom	0	6	12	25	23	14	3	84
Gilroy	1	3	7	12	12	10	4	49
Half Moon Bay	0	0	0	0	0	0	0	0
Laguna Beach	0	0	0	0	0	1	1	3
Long Beach	0	0	0	2	2	3	2	12
Los Ang. Dwntn	1	1	1	3	4	5	3	19
Modesto	1	6	13	24	20	12	2	79
Oakland	0	1	2	1	2	3	1	10
Palmdale	2	7	17	28	27	19	4	104
Palm Springs	12	22	28	31	31	28	19	179
Pasadena	2	2	5	13	15	12	6	57
Redding	1	8	16	28	26	17	5	102
Riverside	3	5	12	24	25	17	8	95
San Diego	0	0	0	0	0	1	1	2
San Rafael	0	2	4	4	4	5	2	21
Santa Barbara	0	0	0	0	0	1	2	5
Stockton	1	6	13	23	21	13	3	80
Thermal	12	22	28	31	31	28	19	178
Tustin	1	1	1	5	7	7	4	28
Walnut Creek	0	3	7	14	14	10	2	50
Yorba Linda	2	2	4	13	14	11	6	54

Source: Western Regional Climate Center Note: Very few winter days go above 90F

In California, almost one acre out of four — some 24 percent — is classified as desert. Most of the desert land is located in Central and Southern California

Average Rain

City	Jan	Mar	May	Jul	Aug	Sep	Nov	Yr. Avg.
Anaheim	3	3	0	0	0	0	1	14
Auburn	7	5	1	0	0	0	4	35
Bakersfield	1	1	0	0	0	0	1	6
Barstow	1	1	0	0	0	0	0	5
Big Bear Lake	4	3	1	1	1	1	2	22
Borrego Springs	1	1	0	0	1	0	1	6
Chula Vista	2	2	0	0	0	0	1	9
Culver City	3	2	0	0	0	0	1	13
Death Valley	0	0	0	0	0	0	0	2
Escondido	3	3	0	0	0	0	2	16
Eureka	7	5	2	0	0	1	6	39
Folsom	5	4	1	0	0	0	3	23
Gilroy	5	3	0	0	0	0	3	21
Half Moon Bay	6	4	1	0	0	0	3	27
Laguna Beach	3	2	0	0	0	0	1	13
Long Beach	3	2	0	0	0	0	1	12
Los Ang. Dwntn	3	2	0	0	0	0	1	15
Modesto	2	2	0	0	0	0	1	13
Oakland	4	2	0	0	0	0	3	18
Palmdale	2	1	0	0	0	0	1	8
Palm Springs	1	1	0	0	0	0	0	6
Pasadena	4	3	0	0	0	0	2	20
Redding	6	8	1	0	0	2	6	44
Riverside	2	2	0	0	0	0	1	10
San Diego	2	2	0	0	0	0	1	10
San Rafael	9	4	1	0	0	0	4	36
Santa Barbara	3	3	0	0	0	0	2	16
Stockton	3	2	0	0	0	0	2	14
Thermal	1	0	0	0	0	0	0	3
Tustin	3	2	0	0	0	0	1	13
Walnut Creek	4	2	0	0	0	0	2	17
Yorba Linda	4	2	0	0	0	0	2	14

Source: Western Regional Climate Center

 The massive General Sherman tree, located in Sequoia National Park, was previously named for whom? (Answer next page).

Death Valley

Second-hottest place in the world (134 degrees in 1913) and one of the driest in the world (1.82 inches average annual rainfall). Its rugged beauty draws over 1 million visitors annually to view Scotty's Castle, the ghost towns, abundant wildlife and petroglyphs.

Approximately 130 miles long and 12 miles wide, Death Valley was declared a National Monument in 1933. In 1994, the park was expanded to take in more desert. The park now covers 3.3 million acres, the largest in the U.S. outside of Alaska.

At 282 feet below sea level, the lowest point in the Western Hemisphere. But a mere 15 miles away, in the Panamint Mountains, towers Telescope Peak, 11,049 feet. Early explorers found lead, gold, silver and borate in the valley. Most left after the ore ran out.

Its name comes from the travails of the first white settlers who in 1849 sought a short cut to the California gold fields. Hungry, thirsty and lost, they wandered through the desert for many days before escaping to name the region "Death Valley."

Only a temperature 2 degrees higher recorded in Northern Africa keeps Death Valley from being the hottest place in the world. The heat, which can kill the unwary, has spawned tall tales including one that a group digging a grave recorded 156 degrees before moving the thermometer to the shade for fear it would break.

Before the name change, the gigantic redwood was named the Karl Marx Tree by early-day socialists who established a colony nearby.

Because of the heat, Death Valley draws most of its visitors from November to mid April. Some of the mountains get a dusting of snow.

Its desolation has lured dozens of movie and television crews to use it as such movies as "Ambush at Stovepipe Wells," "Helter Skelter," "The Twilight Zone" and "Zabriskie Point."

Landmarks and ghost towns dot the region: Surprise Canyon, Badwater, Stovepipe Wells, Coffin Peak, Hell's Gate, Starvation Canyon, Funeral Mountains and Dead Man Pass. Ghost town of Skidoo is legendary for Death Valley's only hanging, Hootch Simpson, a hapless robber who was hanged twice, once for the law and then again for news photographers who missed the first one.

Another colorful character was "Death Valley Scotty," or Walter Scott, a flimflam and former member of Buffalo Bill's Wild West Show. The charming Scott, claiming to own a rich gold mine, convinced a Chicago insurance tycoon to build a $1.5 million "vacation" castle for him in Death Valley. Still standing, the castle is visited annually by thousands of tourists.

Death Valley

 California is the third-largest state in land area behind Alaska and Texas. What state is fourth? (Answer next page).

What's the oldest living thing on earth?

Believe it or not, there are two answers to this question, and both are California residents.

Most often mentioned as the "earth's oldest living inhabitant" is Methuselah, a bristlecone pine, discovered in the White-Inyo Mountains of Eastern California. Dr. Edmund Schulman found the tree in 1957. At that time Schulman calculated the tree to be 4,723 years old. It's now pushing 4,770, making it a seedling at the time of the building of the Great Pyramids.

The precise location of the tree is secret but it is in a remote stand of bristlecone pines, with very little soil or moisture, above the 10,000-foot level in the surreal high desert of the Inyo National Forest. Several of the trees are in the 3,000-4,000 year range. Scientists cloned Methuselah in 2003 as part of the Champion Tree Project.

Not far away, in the extreme climes of the Mojave Desert, grows another curious species, the creosote bush. Native to arid regions of the southwestern United States and South America, this species exhibits an interesting type of growth in which the crown of an individual plant splits into large lobes, some of which then bend back into the soil and develop their own roots and branches. The original dies but the offshoot, with the same DNA, lives on.

According to the Encarta Encyclopedia, one cluster in the Joshua Tree National Forest is estimated to be 11,700 years old, eclipsing Methuselah by nearly 7,000 years.

If you count the traditional way, Methuselah wins the title of oldest. If you accept the DNA approach, creosote is the winner.

 Montana, 147,138 sq. miles, 11,555 sq. miles less than California's 158,693, holds fourth place. The smallest state is Rhode Island with a total of 1,214 sq. miles.

3

Education

Despite financial problems, California boasts one of the finest educational systems in the world.

The system consists of nearly 9,000 public schools with an enrollment exceeding 6 million pupils. Its student body is one of the most diverse in the nation. More than half a million students are enrolled in private schools (also diverse).

Then there are the state's colleges and universities, public and private. Some like Stanford, UCLA, the University of Southern California and UC Berkeley (Cal) lead in academics and athletics.

Others, like the California Institute of Technology, are content with academics.

Both private and public universities have produced Nobel laureates in the fields of medicine, physics and economics, to mention a few.

All benefit the California economy — often subtly, sometimes directly. UC Davis is famous for its wine, vineyard and agricultural research.

California also fields about 106 community colleges and 23 state universities, some with enrollments of about 30,000.

Many students start at the community colleges then transfer into the state universities or the University of California system.

 Name the mascots for the University of California at Irvine and the University of California at Santa Cruz. (Answer next page).

Schools, Enrollments, Teachers
By the Numbers

School Districts	Number
Unified	327
Elementary	566
High	93
Other	70
Total	1,056

Public Schools	Number
Elementary	5,423
Middle	1,171
Junior High	22
High	966
K-12	68
Continuation	521
Alternative	242
Community Day	279
Special Education	122
Other	101
Total	8,915

Students	Number
Kindergarten-8	4,329,008
Grades 9-12	1,745,295
Upgraded programs	73,072
Total	6,147,375

Twelfth-Grade Grads	Number
Total	316,124

Teachers	Number
Elementary	164,670
Middle/Jr. High	50,180
High School	70,911
Other/Continuation	21,179
Total	306,940

Priv. School Students	Number
Total	631,619

Source: California Dept. of Education, 2001-2002 sch. year

The mascot for UC Irvine is the anteater and for UC Santa Cruz, the banana slug.

California's 25 Largest School Districts

District	County	Enrollment
1 Los Angeles USD*	Los Angeles	735,058
2 San Diego City USD	San Diego	141,599
3 Long Beach USD	Los Angeles	96,488
4 Fresno USD	Fresno	81,508
5 Santa Ana USD	Orange	61,909
6 San Francisco USD	San Francisco	58,566
7 San Bernardino USD	San Bernardino	54,166
8 Oakland USD	Alameda	53,545
9 Sacramento City USD	Sacramento	53,418
10 San Juan USD	Sacramento	51,383
11 Elk Grove USD	Sacramento	49,970
12 Garden Grove USD	Orange	49,809
13 Capistrano USD	Orange	46,576
14 Riverside USD	Riverside	39,688
15 Corona-Norco USD	Riverside	39,614
16 Stockton City USD	San Joaquin	39,213
17 Fontana USD	San Bernardino	38,930
18 Sweetwater Union High	San Diego	37,175
19 Mt. Diablo USD	Contra Costa	36,824
20 Montebello USD	Los Angeles	35,379
21 Saddleback Valley USD	Orange	35,117
22 Pomona USD	Los Angeles	35,070
23 West Contra Costa USD	Contra Costa	34,667
24 Clovis USD	Fresno	33,418
25 Moreno Valley USD	Riverside	33,295

Note: These 25 districts enroll about 2 million and count for about a third of all public-school students.

Source: CBEDS, Educational Demographics, 2001-2002 sch. year.

*USD stands for unified school district.

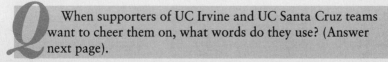

Q When supporters of UC Irvine and UC Santa Cruz teams want to cheer them on, what words do they use? (Answer next page).

25 Smallest School Districts

County	District	Enrollment
Alpine County Office of Ed.	Alpine	3
La Grange Elementary	Stanislaus	7
Panoche Elementary	San Benito	7
Jefferson Elementary	San Benito	10
Lincoln Elementary	Marin	10
Bogus Elementary	Siskiyou	11
Kashia Elementary	Sonoma	11
Mineral Elementary	Tehama	11
Blake Elementary	Kern	13
Green Point Elementary	Humboldt	13
Little Shasta Elementary	Siskiyou	13
Maple Creek Elementary	Humboldt	15
Coffee Creek Elementary	Trinity	15
Ravendale-Termo Elementary	Lassen	15
Forks of Salmon Elementary	Siskiyou	15
Plumas County Office of Education	Plumas	15
Silver Fork Elementary	El Dorado	17
Laguna Joint Elementary	Marin	17
Sierra County Office of Education	Sierra	20
Casmalia Elementary	Santa Barbara	23
French Gulch-Whiskeytown Elem.	Shasta	24
Elkins Elementary	Tehama	24
Cox Bar Elementary	Trinity	24
Chinese Camp Elementary	Tuolumne	26

Source: CBEDS Collection Data, 2001-02 sch. year.

 UC Irvine says "zot,zot,zot" after the anteater, and UC Santa Cruz yells "slime,slime,slime," after the banana slug.

Statewide Teacher Salaries

Elementary School Districts

Statewide Average	Small Dist.	Medium Dist.	Large Dist.
Beginning Teacher	$32,843	$34,611	$35,222
Mid-range Teacher	48,682	48,682	57,707
Highest Teacher	55,974	65,312	70,135
Principal	71,251	80,909	89,033
District Superintendent	90,588	109,512	129,527

High School Districts

Statewide Average	Small	Medium	Large
Beginning Teacher	$32,843	$33,859	$35,124
Mid-range Teacher	48,813	53,134	57,212
Highest Teacher	59,603	67,718	71,349
Principal	76,471	88,469	99,782
District Superintendent	94,630	110,625	138,750

Unified School Districts

Statewide Average	Small	Medium	Large
Beginning Teacher	$31,721	$33,667	$35,146
Mid-range Teacher	46,817	52,075	55,350
Highest Teacher	57,720	65,023	69,221
Principal	71,819	83,920	91,873
District Superintendent	87,290	114,670	148,132

Source: Cal. Dept. of Education, 2000-2001 school year

Q What California college did Richard Nixon attend as an undergraduate student? (Answer next page).

Annual Average Salaries of Public School Teachers
Rankings by State

Rank	State	Salary	Rank	State	Salary
1	New Jersey	$ 53,281	27	New Hampshire	$ 38,301
2	Connecticut	52,693	28	Vermont	38,254
3	California	52,480	29	Florida	38,230
4	New York	52,040	30	Alabama	37,956
5	Michigan	50,694	31	South Carolina	37,938
6	Pennsylvania	49,528	32	Tennessee	37,431
7	Washington D.C.	48,704	33	Missouri	36,722
8	Rhode Island	48,474	34	Kentucky	36,589
9	Alaska	48,123	35	Iowa	36,479
10	Illinois	47,847	36	Utah	36,441
11	Massachusetts	47,789	37	Idaho	36,375
12	Delaware	47,047	38	Maine	36,373
13	Maryland	45,963	39	Arizona	36,302
14	Indiana	43,311	40	Kansas	35,901
15	Ohio	42,764	41	West Virginia	35,888
16	Georgia	42,216	42	Wyoming	34,678
17	Minnesota	42,212	43	Arkansas	34,641
18	Washington	42,137	44	Oklahoma	34,499
19	Wisconsin	42,122	45	Nebraska	34,175
20	Oregon	41,711	46	New Mexico	33,785
21	North Carolina	41,151	47	Louisiana	33,615
22	Nevada	40,443	48	Montana	32,249
23	Virginia	40,197	49	Mississippi	31,954
24	Hawaii	40,052	50	North Dakota	30,891
25	Colorado	39,184	51	South Dakota	30,265
26	Texas	38,361			
				United States	$ 43,335

Source: National Education Association Research, 2000-2001. Some entries are estimates.

Whittier College in Los Angeles County.

California Spending vs. Other States
Amount Spent Per Student, Public Schools

State	Total	State	Total
New York	$ 10,922	Georgia	$ 6,909
New Jersey	10,893	Montana	6,671
Washington D.C.	10,852	Washington	6,613
Connecticut	9,236	Missouri	6,593
Alaska	9,165	South Carolina	6,570
Massachusetts	9,038	Hawaii	6,558
Rhode Island	8,775	Kansas	6,521
Vermont	8,706	Colorado	6,515
Delaware	8,603	Texas	6,460
Pennsylvania	8,191	North Carolina	6,368
Maine	8,178	North Dakota	6,318
Wisconsin	8,158	New Mexico	6,115
Maryland	8,077	Kentucky	6,077
Michigan	8,029	South Dakota	6,063
Wyoming	7,833	Florida	6,020
Illinois	7,585	Oklahoma	6,012
Oregon	7,511	Louisiana	5,934
Ohio	7,499	Arkansas	5,852
West Virginia	7,450	Alabama	5,845
Minnesota	7,447	Nevada	5,778
Indiana	7,287	Tennessee	5,622
Virginia	7,278	Idaho	5,616
New Hampshire	7,065	Mississippi	5,179
California	6,965	Arizona	5,100
Nebraska	6,946	Utah	4,625
Iowa	6,912		
		United States	$ 7,284

Source: Annual Survey of Local Government Finances/U.S. Census Bureau

What Los Angeles County high school was used in the television show, "Beverly Hills 90210"? (Answer next page).

SAT Test Scores By County

County	Enroll.	% Tested	Verbal	Math
Alameda	12,604	52	490	527
Alpine	4	0	0	0
Amador	522	27	534	513
Butte	2,604	29	507	520
Calaveras	576	26	505	516
Colusa	360	23	439	446
Contra Costa	10,607	46	526	545
Del Norte	433	24	505	506
El Dorado	2,194	35	530	548
Fresno	10,432	32	461	481
Glenn	417	30	455	456
Humboldt	1,685	30	521	537
Imperial	2,190	29	426	442
Inyo	250	47	504	507
Kern	9,195	26	481	497
Kings	1,516	21	469	469
Lake	700	25	498	509
Lassen	390	33	473	476
Los Angeles	88,352	40	468	497
Madera	1,620	17	481	494
Marin	2,033	59	544	556
Mariposa	214	28	537	545
Mendocino	1,178	33	530	528
Merced	3,625	22	462	475
Modoc	185	18	494	511
Mono	142	43	522	498
Monterey	3,871	35	451	465
Napa	1,388	32	514	524
Nevada	1,055	38	535	536

Torrance High School, located in the City of Torrance, about 15 miles south of Beverly Hills.

SAT Test Scores By County

County	Enroll.	% Tested	Verbal	Math
Orange	30,706	42	515	554
Placer	4,503	33	518	531
Plumas	271	38	513	501
Riverside	19,644	31	471	488
Sacramento	13,817	32	488	512
San Benito	621	38	463	481
San Bernardino	21,934	30	473	491
San Diego	30,465	41	499	519
San Francisco	4,315	60	464	522
San Joaquin	7,827	26	471	494
San Luis Obispo	2,907	32	527	537
San Mateo	5,542	48	501	534
Santa Barbara	4,048	33	516	533
Santa Clara	16,431	49	514	556
Santa Cruz	2,814	36	515	533
Shasta	2,456	23	523	532
Sierra	79	51	490	479
Siskiyou	578	26	497	503
Solano	4,754	32	486	506
Sonoma	4,873	35	529	539
Stanislaus	6,495	22	497	514
Sutter	1,132	24	497	522
Tehama	778	22	498	504
Trinity	190	30	507	513
Tulare	5,573	24	463	479
Tuolumne	596	30	536	536
Ventura	9,257	32	519	538
Yolo	2,004	39	543	564
Yuba	955	15	452	483
Statewide:	365,907	37	490	516

Source: California Dept. of Education, 2002 .

Q What famous university owes its life to the death of a boy? (Answer next page).

Who's Going to College — By County

County	H.S. Grads	UC	CSU	Com. Coll.	Total
Alameda	12,648	1,618	1,746	4,694	8,058
Alpine	1	0	0	1	1
Amador	422	18	37	87	142
Butte	2,048	79	354	850	1,283
Calaveras	446	22	42	138	202
Colusa	284	7	50	56	113
Contra Costa	9,927	1,058	1,120	2,032	4,210
Del Norte	303	14	29	77	120
El Dorado	1,800	94	201	623	918
Fresno	9,518	368	1,282	913	2,563
Glenn	388	14	70	149	233
Humboldt	1,440	63	183	460	706
Imperial	1,998	78	108	973	1,159
Inyo	278	13	20	57	90
Kern	8,501	251	756	2,624	3,631
Kings	1,294	35	93	328	456
Lake	520	21	39	121	181
Lassen	331	3	8	98	109
Los Angeles	88,471	7,748	9,986	26,154	43,888
Madera	1,243	49	121	141	311
Marin	2,290	346	281	456	1,083
Mariposa	180	5	3	51	59
Mendocino	1,062	57	80	368	505
Merced	3,097	103	279	988	1,370
Modoc	176	3	11	24	38
Mono	143	7	8	27	42
Monterey	3,761	219	380	485	1,084
Napa	1,347	94	141	288	523
Nevada	1,138	73	103	322	498
Orange	30,091	2,855	2,916	11,071	16,842

A Stanford. *Upon the death of their 15-year-old son from typhoid, Leland and Jane Stanford devoted their energies to building the university, which was named after the boy, Leland Stanford Jr.*

Who's Going to College — By County

County	H.S. Grads	UC	CSU	Com. Coll.	Total
Placer	3,890	206	361	1,235	1,802
Plumas	276	8	13	93	114
Riverside	16,929	1,077	1,333	3,149	5,559
Sacramento	12,707	845	1,544	4,813	7,202
San Benito	624	27	71	205	303
San Bernardino	19,676	985	1,780	5,890	8,655
San Diego	27,757	2,168	2,992	7,444	12,604
San Francisco	5,106	944	887	1,105	2,936
San Joaquin	6,323	281	542	2,168	2,991
San Luis Obispo	2,497	152	267	1,048	1,467
San Mateo	5,951	672	778	1,928	3,378
Santa Barbara	3,886	327	250	1,529	2,106
Santa Clara	15,822	2,044	2,323	3,212	7,579
Santa Cruz	2,619	317	236	636	1,189
Shasta	2,053	52	109	754	915
Sierra	46	2	10	3	15
Siskiyou	527	26	45	86	157
Solano	4,351	241	454	1,283	1,978
Sonoma	4,600	340	477	1,884	2,701
Stanislaus	5,562	188	530	2,224	2,942
Sutter	954	20	80	271	371
Tehama	652	16	61	240	317
Trinity	185	3	21	68	92
Tulare	4,405	140	336	1,845	2,321
Tuolumne	593	34	49	226	309
Ventura	8,447	568	547	3,995	5,110
Yolo	1,759	276	187	490	953
Yuba	780	11	38	170	219
Total	344,123	27,285	36,768	102,650	166,703

Source: California Postsecondary Education Commission, 2001-02 academic year

 Although it is located in a fairly dry area, the next University of California campus was forced to pick a new site because of water. Why? (Answer next page).

Who's Going To College — Men & Women

County	UC Men	UC Women	CSU Men	CSU Women	Com. Coll. Men	Com. Coll. Women
Alameda	593	739	664	820	2,159	2,166
Amador	9	9	15	22	43	44
Butte	37	42	149	201	414	431
Calaveras	11	11	17	25	62	75
Colusa	2	5	19	31	28	28
Contra Costa	385	569	411	560	904	959
Del Norte	5	8	12	17	31	35
El Dorado	47	47	85	116	315	305
Fresno	146	207	445	774	366	464
Glenn	3	11	28	42	75	74
Humboldt	29	33	66	108	201	239
Imperial	36	40	33	72	437	522
Inyo	3	10	8	12	24	30
Kern	103	131	267	454	1,272	1,295
Kings	20	15	34	59	166	155
Lake	7	14	10	29	63	57
Lassen	2	1	4	4	50	48
Los Angeles	2,733	3,724	3,309	4,847	11,648	12,478
Madera	22	27	56	64	63	77
Marin	101	164	108	120	246	192
Mariposa	3	2	2	1	26	25
Mendocino	22	32	33	45	186	180
Merced	37	66	84	192	477	509
Modoc	1	2	5	6	12	12
Mono	1	6	3	5	20	6
Monterey	73	84	146	182	240	208
Napa	32	41	45	71	117	124
Nevada	36	35	36	60	148	155
Orange	1,191	1,373	1,118	1,561	5,338	5,228

 The university is to be located near Merced, in an area dotted with wetlands, important for wild life. After the first site ran into oppostion, another site was found.

Who's Going To College — Men & Women

County	UC Men	UC Women	CSU Men	CSU Women	Com. Coll. Men	Com. Coll. Women
Placer	84	121	156	205	588	626
Plumas	6	2	2	11	47	40
Riverside	443	589	531	753	1,337	1,687
Sacramento	278	421	514	797	2,249	2,351
San Benito	10	17	27	44	97	108
San Bernardino	414	519	691	1,011	2,614	3,099
San Diego	880	1,130	1,136	1,670	3,438	3,749
San Francisco	270	371	283	329	477	447
San Joaquin	99	156	171	318	1,009	1,040
San Luis Obispo	56	87	106	151	482	542
San Mateo	235	287	290	317	894	877
Santa Barbara	117	161	101	99	692	709
Santa Clara	791	938	882	1,059	1,524	1,423
Santa Cruz	104	162	88	126	301	263
Shasta	17	29	37	71	372	376
Sierra	1	1	5	5	2	1
Siskiyou	14	12	22	23	41	45
Solano	90	122	174	245	587	660
Sonoma	153	161	165	239	875	885
Stanislaus	63	102	157	337	991	1,128
Sutter	12	8	36	44	126	142
Tehama	5	5	23	30	98	136
Trinity	0	3	7	14	36	32
Tulare	53	85	140	191	844	977
Tuolumne	18	16	20	29	101	119
Ventura	231	283	195	308	1,802	1,926
Yolo	131	145	80	107	238	251
Yuba	1	8	15	22	59	92

Source: California Postsecondary Education Commission, 2001-2002 sch. year.

 The Bancroft library at UC Berkeley is one of the largest in the world. It includes how many volumes? (Answer next page).

Who's Going To a UC by Ethnic Group
Public School Grads 19 & Under

County	Asian	Af.Am.	Filipino	Hisp.	Nat. Am.	White
Alameda	621	44	58	93	7	359
Amador	1	0	1	0	0	15
Butte	7	0	1	4	1	62
Calaveras	2	0	0	2	0	16
Colusa	0	0	0	4	0	3
Contra Costa	268	30	46	74	8	439
Del Norte	2	0	0	2	0	8
El Dorado	8	0	0	5	0	69
Fresno	108	8	6	67	4	131
Glenn	2	0	0	3	0	8
Humboldt	4	0	1	4	1	46
Imperial	11	1	0	48	1	12
Inyo	0	0	0	2	1	10
Kern	42	8	21	44	4	99
Kings	0	1	2	8	0	18
Lake	2	0	0	3	0	12
Lassen	0	0	0	0	0	3
Los Angeles	2,906	299	256	1,179	20	1,271
Madera	9	3	1	11	2	21
Marin	31	3	2	19	3	179
Mariposa	0	0	0	0	0	5
Mendocino	3	0	0	4	0	39
Merced	27	2	3	36	1	26
Modoc	0	0	0	1	1	1
Mono	1	0	0	0	0	6
Monterey	29	3	8	47	2	56
Napa	6	0	3	6	1	52
Nevada	3	0	0	1	0	58
Orange	1,149	31	69	209	15	838

The Bancroft library holds more than 500,000 volumes, along with millions of manuscripts and photographs.

Who's Going To UC by Ethnic Group
Public School Grads 19 & Under

County	Asian	Af.Am.	Filipino	Hisp.	Nat. Am.	White
Placer	18	8	3	7	0	149
Plumas	1	0	0	0	0	7
Riverside	162	34	69	276	10	422
Sacramento	252	25	23	62	15	269
San Benito	1	0	2	10	0	12
San Bernardino	203	57	53	248	8	291
San Diego	346	73	215	268	7	905
San Francisco	469	10	27	20	0	76
San Joaquin	85	6	27	22	1	103
San Luis Obispo	8	1	0	16	2	105
San Mateo	198	4	38	44	1	198
Santa Barbara	24	3	11	69	0	148
Santa Clara	985	20	55	78	5	421
Santa Cruz	20	2	2	29	4	183
Shasta	4	0	0	1	0	37
Sierra	0	0	0	0	0	1
Siskiyou	2	1	1	2	0	18
Solano	40	10	32	35	2	86
Sonoma	23	3	7	20	1	231
Stanislaus	39	3	5	17	1	76
Sutter	5	0	0	5	0	10
Tehama	1	0	1	0	0	8
Trinity	0	0	0	0	0	3
Tulare	19	1	7	49	1	53
Tuolumne	1	1	0	1	0	26
Ventura	104	8	27	82	4	241
Yolo	44	2	1	33	3	169
Yuba	4	2	0	0	0	3
Total:	8,300	707	1,084	3,270	137	8,113

Source: California Postsecondary Education Commission, 2001-2 school year.

Note: 1,891 students did not list an ethnic category

 Several elements on the Periodic Table were discovered and named by scientists at UC Berkeley and two have a distinct California flavor. They are: (Answer next page).

Top 100 High Schools by Math SAT

High School	City	County	Average Math Score	Average Verbal Score
Whitney High	Cerritos	Los Angeles	684	643
Monta Vista High	Cupertino	Santa Clara	664	588
Lynbrook High	San Jose	Santa Clara	662	577
San Marino High	San Marino	Los Angeles	651	573
Gunn High	Palo Alto	Santa Clara	649	593
University High	Irvine	Orange	643	578
Saratoga High	Saratoga	Santa Clara	640	593
Palo Alto High	Palo Alto	Santa Clara	640	612
Lowell High	San Francisco	San Francisco	636	591
Mission San Jose High	Fremont	Alameda	632	574
Arcadia High	Arcadia	Los Angeles	630	545
Troy High	Fullerton	Orange	629	585
Palos Verdes Peninsula	Rolling Hills Est.	Los Angeles	619	557
South Pasadena	So. Pasadena	Los Angeles	618	560
Davis High	Davis	Yolo	613	587
Campolindo High	Moraga	Contra Costa	610	587
Cupertino High	Cupertino	Santa Clara	609	531
Sunny Hills High	Fullerton	Orange	608	537
Torrey Pines High	San Diego	San Diego	608	565
Miramonte High	Orinda	Contra Costa	607	590
Calif. Acad. Math/Science	Carson	Los Angeles	607	568
Piedmont High	Piedmont	Alameda	604	588
Homestead High	Cupertino	Santa Clara	604	545
Albany High	Albany	Alameda	603	551
Acalanes High	Lafayette	Contra Costa	603	579
La Cañada High	La Cañ-Flintridge	Los Angeles	602	558
Leland High	San Jose	Santa Clara	601	551
Mira Loma High	Sacramento	Sacramento	600	571
Rio Americano High	Sacramento	Sacramento	599	571
Northgate High	Walnut Creek	Contra Costa	597	564
Beverly Hills High	Beverly Hills	Los Angeles	597	549
Wilson (Glen A.) High	Hacienda Hts.	Los Angeles	597	523
Cerritos High	Cerritos	Los Angeles	594	509
Irvine High	Irvine	Orange	594	536

 Berkelium (BK), Californium (CF), Lawrencium (LR), Seaborgium (SG). Ernest Lawrence and Glen Seaborg, Nobel winners, were members of the UC faculty.

Top 100 High Schools by Math SAT (cont.)

School Name	City	County	Average Math Score	Average Verbal Score
Calabasas High	Calabasas	Los Angeles	592	559
Woodbridge High	Irvine	Orange	591	543
Northwood High	Irvine	Orange	591	541
La Jolla High	La Jolla	San Diego	591	568
San Ramon Valley High	Danville	Contra Costa	590	558
Owens Valley High	Independence	Inyo	590	588
Redwood High	Larkspur	Marin	589	557
Mountain View High	Mountain View	Santa Clara	589	553
Los Gatos High	Los Gatos	Santa Clara	588	564
Los Altos High	Los Altos	Santa Clara	588	544
Foothill High	Pleasanton	Alameda	587	550
Monte Vista High	Danville	Contra Costa	587	559
Corona Del Mar High	Newport Beach	Orange	586	558
Thousand Oaks High	Thousand Oaks	Ventura	586	553
Diamond Bar High	Diamond Bar	Los Angeles	585	522
Las Lomas High	Walnut Creek	Contra Costa	584	558
Temple City High	Temple City	Los Angeles	584	494
Clark Magnet High	La Crescenta	Los Angeles	583	517
Southern Trinity High	Bridgeville	Trinity	583	518
Aliso Niguel High	Aliso Viejo	Orange	582	543
Crescenta Valley High	La Crescenta	Los Angeles	580	523
West High	Torrance	Los Angeles	580	512
Pacific Collegiate	Santa Cruz	Santa Cruz	580	567
Santa Cruz High	Santa Cruz	Santa Cruz	580	562
Westlake High	Westlake Village	Ventura	579	555
Ponderosa High	Shingle Springs	El Dorado	578	548
Bella Vista High	Fair Oaks	Sacramento	578	559
Etna Junior High	Etna	Siskiyou	578	596
California High	San Ramon	Contra Costa	577	543
Agoura High	Agoura	Los Angeles	577	556
Van Nuys High	Van Nuys	Los Angeles	577	540
Amador Valley High	Pleasanton	Alameda	576	544
Mark Keppel High	Alhambra	Los Angeles	576	544
Hart Senior High	Newhall	Los Angeles	576	554

 When professors at UC Berkeley win a Nobel, the University awards them: the Berkeley Nobellium, a rare honor; $100,000; $200,000; free parking space. (Answer next page).

Top 100 High Schools by Math SAT (cont.)

School Name	City	County	Average Math Score	Average Verbal Score
La Costa Canyon High	Encinitas	San Diego	575	534
San Mateo High	San Mateo	San Mateo	575	519
Fall River High	McArthur	Shasta	575	521
Analy High	Sebastopol	Sonoma	575	564
Dana Hills High	Dana Point	Orange	574	566
Harbor High	Santa Cruz	Santa Cruz	574	538
Walnut High	Walnut	Los Angeles	572	509
Dos Pueblos High	Goleta	Santa Barbara	572	539
Marina High	Huntington Bch.	Orange	571	529
Laguna Hills High	Laguna Hills	Orange	571	540
Capistrano Valley High	Mission Viejo	Orange	570	529
High Tech High	San Diego	San Diego	570	610
Brea-Olinda High	Brea	Orange	569	513
Esperanza High	Anaheim	Orange	569	536
El Dorado High	Placentia	Orange	569	542
Morro Bay High	Morro Bay	San Luis Obispo	569	540
Oak Park High	Oak Park	Ventura	569	544
South High	Torrance	Los Angeles	568	509
Aragon High	San Mateo	San Mateo	568	535
Berkeley High	Berkeley	Alameda	567	544
Foothill High	Santa Ana	Orange	567	531
Granada High	Livermore	Alameda	566	533
Rancho Bernardo High	Poway	San Diego	566	530
El Molino High	Forestville	Sonoma	566	568
Mills High	Millbrae	San Mateo	565	516
Saugus High	Saugus	Los Angeles	564	534
Fountain Valley High	Fountain Val.	Orange	564	520
Villa Park High	Villa Park	Orange	564	531
El Toro High	Lake Forest	Orange	564	533
Poway High	Poway	San Diego	564	535
Camarillo High	Camarillo	Ventura	563	534
College Park High	Pleasant Hill	Contra Costa	562	543
Claremont High	Claremont	Los Angeles	562	528

Source: Cal. Dept. of Education 2002

Free parking, which in parking-starved, ticket-happy Berkeley, is quite an honor.

Community Colleges
Fingertip Facts

- The California Community College system consists of 108 colleges around the state.
- In fall, 2002, the colleges enrolled 1.7 million students, full time, part time and occasional. Yearly enrollment runs about 2.9 million, making the system the largest in higher education in the world.
- Like many college systems these days, women outnumber men. In fall 2002, the community colleges counted 973,640 women students and 755,109 men students. The college system reported that 17,977 students did not identify themselves by any sex.
- The colleges serve residents across a wide spectrum of ages. In 2002, 1,055,641 students were 29 years of age or younger, 479,092 students fell between the ages of 30 and 49, and 205,355 students were 50 or older.
- The ethnic variety is also diverse. In 2002, 211,170 students were Asian, 124,889 were African-American, 56,902 were Filipino, 473,232 were Hispanic, 15,629 were Native American and 11,091 were Pacific Islander.

Transfers from California Community Colleges to State and Private Universities

Year	CSU	UC	Private Univ.
1996	48,688	10,886	7,526
1997	48,349	10,492	7,673
1998	45,546	10,210	7,950
1999	44,989	10,161	8,080
2000	47,706	10,827	8,442
2001	47,900	11,215	NA

Source: California Postsecondary Education Commission

 What event in 1933 forced extensive redesigns in California schools? (Answer next page).

California State Universities

Campus	Undergrads	*Cert.	Grads	Total
Bakersfield	5,595	1,388	782	7,765
Channel Islands	495	135	0	630
Chico	14,264	970	1,012	16,246
Dominguez Hills	8,041	2,361	3,102	13,504
Fresno	17,309	2,025	1,938	21,272
Fullerton	26,434	2,009	3,700	32,143
Hayward	9,703	1,694	2,479	13,876
Humboldt	6,566	523	522	7,611
Long Beach	27,863	2,923	3,780	34,566
Los Angeles	14,294	2,388	4,417	21,099
Maritime Acad.	704	17	0	721
Monterey Bay	3,153	292	106	3,551
Northridge	25,781	3,981	3,817	33,579
Pomona	17,403	1,307	1,111	19,821
Sacramento	22,564	2,345	3,649	28,558
San Bernardino	11,255	2,787	2,299	16,341
San Diego	27,846	1,595	4,863	34,304
San Francisco	20,828	2,621	4,929	28,378
San Jose	22,152	2,259	5,939	30,350
San Luis Obispo	17,401	277	775	18,453
San Marcos	6,149	973	556	7,678
Sonoma	6,734	936	549	8,219
Stanislaus	5,867	1,299	684	7,850
Totals	318,401	37,105	51,009	406,515
Int'l Programs	532	20	21	573
Grand Totals	318,933	37,125	51,030	407,088

*Cert. Certificate programs, many of them for teaching degrees.
Source: CSU System, 2002

A *The Long Beach earthquake killed 120 people, caused about $50 million damage and toppled schools, prompting tougher standards for school construction.*

University of California Overview

University	Est.	Acres	Undergrads	Grads	Total
Berkeley	1868	1,600	22,398	8,613	31,011
Davis	1908	5,200	19,460	5,632	25,092
Irvine	1964	1,400	14,533	3,633	18,166
Los Angeles	1919	419	24,103	11,693	35,796
Riverside	1954	1,160	9,281	1,321	10,602
San Diego	1959	2,124	15,925	3,422	19,347
San Francisco	1873	163	36	3,475	3,511
Santa Barbara	1944	989	17,068	2,295	19,363
Santa Cruz	1965	2,950	9,960	1,021	10,981

Source: UC 2001

 What California university does not have a campus in the Golden State? (Answer next page).

Educational Attainment

	U.S.		CA	
	Number	Percent	Number	Percent
Less than 9th grade	13,755,477	8%	2,446,324	12%
9th to 12th, no diploma	21,960,148	12%	2,496,419	12%
HS Graduate & equiv.	52,168,981	29%	4,288,452	20%
Some College, no degree	38,351,595	21%	4,879,336	23%
Associate Degree	11,512,833	6%	1,518,403	7%
Bachelor's Degree	28,317,792	16%	3,640,157	17%
Graduate or Prof. Degree	16,144,813	9%	2,029,809	10%
% H.S. Graduate or Higher		80%		77%
% Bachelor's Degree or Higher		24%		27%

Source: Population Survey Report 2001 Dept. of Finance, Demographics Research Unit

California University of Pennsylvania, located in the town of California, Pennsylvania.

Median Personal Income by Years of School
Men and Women

Attainment:	Total	Men	Women
Elementary	$9,200	$14,300	$6,700
Some High School	$11,100	$17,500	$7,600
High School Graduate	$18,900	$25,000	$13,000
Some College	$27,000	$33,700	$21,500
Associate	$30,000	$39,300	$23,200
Bachelor's	$38,200	$50,000	$32,200
Master's	$49,500	$66,700	$41,000
Professional*	$70,300	$83,300	$57,100
Doctorate	$62,700	$70,000	$37,300
Total	$23,300	$30,400	$16,000

*Professional degrees include MD, DDS, LLB, and JD

Source: Population Survey, 2001, California Dept. of Finance

 Linus Pauling, the California Institute of Technology in Pasadena, won a Nobel in 1954 for chemistry. In 1962, he won a second Nobel that brought him applause and criticism. It was for? (Answer next page).

Persons With a High School Diploma or Higher
Men and Women by Age

Ages	Males	% of Age	Females	% of Age	Total	% of Age
25-34	2,060,000	82	2,177,000	84	4,237,000	83
35-49	3,371,000	84	3,453,000	83	6,824,000	83
50-64	1,854,000	83	1,865,000	80	3,719,000	81
65+	1,147,000	75	1,431,000	72	2,578,000	73
Total	8,432,000	82	8,926,000	80	17,358,000	81

Source: Population Survey, 2001, California Dept. of Finance, people over age 25.

Persons with a BA/BS Degree or Higher
Men and Women by Age

Ages	Males	% of Age	Females	% of Age	Total	% of Age
25-34	696,000	27.7	825,000	31.8	1,520,000	29.7
35-49	1,271,000	31.5	1,255,000	30.2	2,526,000	30.8
50-64	821,000	36.8	654,000	27.9	1,475,000	32.2
65+	380,000	24.8	303,000	15.2	683,000	19.4
Total	3,168,000	30.7	3,036,000	27.4	6,204,000	29.0

Source: Population Survey, 2001, California Dept. of Finance, people over age 25.

A Pauling won the 1962 Nobel for peace. He was a pacifist and repeatedly warned of the dangers of nuclear war and nuclear fallout. His positions put him at odds with people who thought a nuclear deterrent was necessary.

2003 Distinguished Middle & High Schools

School Name	City	County
Albany Middle	Albany	Alameda
Canyon Middle	Castro Valley	Alameda
Dublin High	Dublin	Alameda
Wells Middle	Dublin	Alameda
Mission San Jose High	Fremont	Alameda
William Mendenhall Middle	Livermore	Alameda
Thomas S. Hart Middle	Pleasanton	Alameda
Las Lomas High	Walnut Creek	Contra Costa
Excelsior School	Byron	Contra Costa
Foothill Middle	Walnut Creek	Contra Costa
Valley View Middle	Pleasant Hill	Contra Costa
Union Mine High	El Dorado	El Dorado
Miller's Hill Elementary	Shingle Springs	El Dorado
Clovis High	Clovis	Fresno
Clovis West High	Fresno	Fresno
Edison Computech 7-8	Fresno	Fresno
Foothill Middle	Prather	Fresno
Winship Middle	Eureka	Humboldt
McKinleyville High	McKinleyville	Humboldt
Toddy Thomas Elementary	Fortuna	Humboldt
Imperial High	Imperial	Imperial
Tevis Junior High	Bakersfield	Kern
Murray Middle	Ridgecrest	Kern
Middletown High	Middletown	Lake
Lassen High	Susanville	Lassen
Carmenita Middle	Cerritos	Los Angeles
Whitney High	Cerritos	Los Angeles
Mayfair High	Lakewood	Los Angeles
Beverly Hills High	Beverly Hills	Los Angeles
Bonita High	La Verne	Los Angeles
San Dimas High	San Dimas	Los Angeles
El Roble Intermediate	Claremont	Los Angeles
El Segundo High	El Segundo	Los Angeles
Rosemont Middle	La Crescenta	Los Angeles

 What California novelist, now enjoying a revival, won the Nobel prize for literature in 1962?

2003 Distinguished Middle & High Schools (Cont.)

School Name	City	County
La Cañada High	La Cañada-Flintridge	Los Angeles
Avalon High	Santa Catalina	Los Angeles
CA Acad. of Math. & Science	Carson	Los Angeles
Stanford Middle	Long Beach	Los Angeles
Paul Revere Charter Middle	Los Angeles	Los Angeles
Robert A. Millikan Mid./Perf. Arts	Sherman Oaks	Los Angeles
Arlie F. Hutchinson Middle	La Mirada	Los Angeles
Miraleste Intermediate	Palos Verdes	Los Angeles
Palos Verdes Intermediate	Palos Verdes Estates	Los Angeles
Palos Verdes Pennisula High	Rolling Hills Estates	Los Angeles
Diamond Ranch High	Pomona	Los Angeles
Jefferson Middle	Torrance	Los Angeles
Malibu High	Malibu	Los Angeles
Casimir Middle	Torrance	Los Angeles
J. H. Hull Middle	Torrance	Los Angeles
Madrona Middle	Torrance	Los Angeles
South High	Torrance	Los Angeles
La Serna High	Whittier	Los Angeles
Oak Creek Intermediate	Oakhurst	Madera
San Jose Middle	Novato	Marin
Sinaloa Middle	Novato	Marin
Del Mar Middle	Tiburon	Marin
Redwood High	Larkspur	Marin
River Middle School	Napa	Napa
Brea Junior High	Brea	Orange
Parks Junior High	Fullerton	Orange
Ethel R. Dwyer Middle	Huntington Beach	Orange
Fountain Valley High	Fountain Valley	Orange
Thurston Middle	Laguna Beach	Orange
McAuliffe Middle	Los Alamitos	Orange
Bernardo Yorba Middle	Yorba Linda	Orange
Esperanza High	Anaheim	Orange
La Paz Intermediate	Mission Viejo	Orange
Los Alisos Intermediate	Mission Viejo	Orange

 John Steinbeck, author of such classics as "Grapes of Wrath," "East of Eden," and "Cannery Row."

2003 Distinguished Middle & High Schools (Cont.)

School Name	City	County
Douglas MacArthur Fund. Interm.	Santa Ana	Orange
Pioneer Middle	Tustin	Orange
Trabuco Hills High*	Mission Viejo	Orange
Silverado Middle	Roseville	Placer
Granite Oaks Middle	Rocklin	Placer
Norco High*	Norco	Riverside
Norco Intermediate	Norco	Riverside
La Quinta High	La Quinta	Riverside
Palm Desert Middle	Palm Desert	Riverside
Bella Vista High	Fair Oaks	Sacramento
Rancho Cucamonga High	Etiwanda	San Bernardino
Grace Yokley Middle	Ontario	San Bernardino
Joan MacQueen Middle	Alpine	San Diego
Norman L. Sullivan Middle	Bonsall	San Diego
Hillsdale Middle	El Cajon	San Diego
Aviara Oaks Middle	Carlsbad	San Diego
Carlsbad High	Carlsbad	San Diego
Coronado High*	Coronado	San Diego
Coronado Middle	Coronado	San Diego
El Camino High	Oceanside	San Diego
Jefferson Middle	Oceanside	San Diego
Gaspar De Portola Middle	Tarzana	San Diego
La Jolla High	La Jolla	San Diego
Thurgood Marshall Middle	San Diego	San Diego
William H. Standley Middle	San Diego	San Diego
Carmel Valley Middle	San Diego	San Diego
Diegueno Middle	Encinitas	San Diego
Earl Warren Middle	Solana Beach	San Diego
Guajome Park Academy, Inc.	Vista	San Diego
Rancho Buena Vista High	Vista	San Diego
Gateway High	San Francisco	San Francisco
Raoul Wallenberg Traditional High	San Francisco	San Francisco
School of the Arts	San Francisco	San Francisco
Merrill F. West High	Tracy	San Joaquin

Name the first African-American elected to a state-wide office in California.

2003 Distinguished Middle & High Schools (Cont.)

School Name	City	County
Templeton Middle	Templeton	San Luis Obispo
Burlingame Intermediate	Burlingame	San Mateo
William H. Crocker Middle	Hillsborough	San Mateo
Ernest Righetti High	Santa Maria	Santa Barbara
Piedmont Middle	San Jose	Santa Clara
Sierramont Middle	San Jose	Santa Clara
Leigh High	San Jose	Santa Clara
Piedmont Hills High	San Jose	Santa Clara
Chaboya Middle	San Jose	Santa Clara
Homestead High	Cupertino	Santa Clara
Lynbrook High	San Jose	Santa Clara
Monta Vista High	Cupertino	Santa Clara
Mountain View High	Mountain View	Santa Clara
Bernal Intermediate	San Jose	Santa Clara
Leonard Herman Intermed.	San Jose	Santa Clara
John Muir Middle	San Jose	Santa Clara
Leland High*	San Jose	Santa Clara
Foothill High	Palo Cedro	Shasta
Loyalton High	Loyalton	Sierra
Charles L. Sullivan Middle	Fairfield	Solano
Mountain Shadows Middle	Rohnert Park	Sonoma
Altimira Middle	Sonoma	Sonoma
Hickman Middle	Hickman	Stanislaus
La Loma Junior High	Modesto	Stanislaus
Salida Middle	Salida	Stanislaus
Corning High	Corning	Tehama
Tulare Union High	Tulare	Tulare
Los Cerritos Middle	Thousand Oaks	Ventura
Westlake High	Westlake Village	Ventura
Moorpark High	Moorpark	Ventura
Esparto Middle	Esparto	Yolo

* Denotes exemplary career technical education schools.

Source: Calif. Dept. of Education

 Wilson Riles, state superintendent of schools, 1971-1983.

Enrollment in and Number of Public Schools by Grade Span

Grade	Number	Enrollment	Grade	Number	Enrollment
Elementary Schools			**Junior High Schools**		
Kdgn	13	2,612	7-9	14	14,790
K-1	20	5,641	Other*	8	4,520
K-2	56	22,571	Total	22	19,310
K-3	106	45,852			
K-4	99	50,250	**Kindergarten - 12 Schools**		
K-5	2,326	1,468,983			
K-6	1,977	1,223,225	K-12	39	32,936
K-7	36	12,574	Other*	29	5,039
K-8	585	240,006	Total	68	37,975
1-5	14	8,174			
1-6	12	5,535	**Community Day Schools**		
1-8	8	1,550			
3-5	34	17,810	1-6	7	124
3-6	15	6,819	4-6	6	28
3-8	7	2,726	5-8	9	90
4-5	12	5,943	6-8	13	139
4-6	23	12,727	10-12	7	83
4-8	19	8,659	7-8	31	445
Other*	61	21,054	7-9	6	53
Total	5,423	3,162,711	7-10	7	242
			7-11	9	205
Middle Schools			7-12	24	2,312
4-8	20	11,920	8-8	9	51
5-8	43	38,721	8-10	6	51
6-8	768	779,243	8-11	7	90
7-8	309	272,766	8-12	16	446
Other*	31	15,976	9-11	10	88
Total	1,171	1,118,626	9-12	28	1,653
			Other*	84	2,470
			Total	279	8,570

Source: Cal. Dept . of Ed. 2001-02

 The University of California is one of the largest employers in the state. It employs:
A. 100,000-125,000
B. 125,000-150,000
C. 150,000-175,000
(Answer next page).

Enrollment in and Number of Public Schools
by Grade Span *(cont.)*

Grade	Number	Enrollment
Alternative Schools		
K-8	21	3,695
K-12	61	22,388
1-12	15	2,412
7-12	18	7,419
8-12	8	1,003
9-12	57	16,331
10-12	7	974
Other*	55	5,136
Total	242	59,358
High Schools		
6-12	8	9,194
7-12	38	26,246
8-12	16	31,743
9-9	12	1,569
9-10	7	3,591
9-11	15	5,930
9-12	846	1,511,651
Other*	24	12,382
Total	966	1,602,306
Continuation High Schools		
7-12	17	4,256
8-12	11	2,201
9-10	9	211
9-11	18	376
9-12	293	43,057
10-12	119	12,281
11-12	25	1,723
Other*	29	4,770

Grade	Number	Enrollment
Special Education Schools		
Total	521	68,875
Kdgn.	6	45
K-12	40	17,934
Other*	76	11,745
Total	122	29,724
All Other School Types		
K-12	11	13,344
1-12	6	3,807
5-12	6	2,647
6-12	12	3,034
7-12	22	4,324
9-12	18	4,231
Other*	26	8,533
Total	101	39,920
State Totals		
All Schools	8,915	6,147,375

*Schools with various grade spans that are less common.

Source: Cal. Dept. of Education, 2001-02

A *The University of California employs 167,199 full and part-time employees.*

4

Politics & History

California History and Highlights

An American general credited his victories to getting to battle with the "firstest and the mostest" — first in the field with the most men. The conquest of California proved the second half of this dictum.

Spain was first. In 1542, Juan Cabrillo sailed into San Diego Bay and then north to the Mendocino Coast. Other explorers followed, including Francis Drake, the English pirate, who gave England a claim to California.

All missed San Francisco Bay, possibly because of coastal fogs. Had the Bay been discovered earlier, California's history might have turned out much differently. In the days of sailing ships, sheltered bays were highly prized. San Francisco has one of the best natural harbors in the world.

Spain remained foremost in explorations but its attention was diverted by internal arguments over control of the missions and its conquest of the Philippines. Here was an El Dorado of goods, trade and treasure. In the mid-1700s, however, concerned about the English, Dutch and Russian excursions, Spain moved to colonize California.

In 1769, land and sea expeditions reached San Diego, and later that year, traveling by land, Gaspar de Portola and his men discovered San Francisco Bay. Missions were established,

 One of the most treasured exhibits of the Ronald Reagan museum in Simi Valley is an ugly slab of concrete. Why is it cherished? (Answer next page).

Napoleon

forts and pubelos built, and plans laid to bring in more colonists. A few more did come, traveling overland through Colorado. But in 1781, the Yuma Indians wiped out two missions along this route, effectively closing it until 1823.

Meanwhile, Napoleon was raising havoc with Spain and with its New World possessions. In 1803, Napoleon, to raise money for his wars, sold the middle of America to the United States — the Louisiana Purchase. Napoleon also invaded Spain, disrupting its imperial ambitions, and planted the idea of freedom throughout the world. In 1821, following the example of many South American countries, Mexico declared her independence, and took over the Spanish claim to California.

Mexico opened mission lands to ranching, which helped the economy, but did not bring in more settlers. At the eve of the Mexican-American War, which started over Texas, fewer than 7,000 "Californios" populated the land. The Yankees, who had been immigrating into California for several years and who had Navy and Army forces to help them, did not so much defeat the Californios as overwhelm them with numbers — the "mostest" carried the day.

In 1848, the same year that the treaty was signed, gold was discovered in the Sierra and a mad rush to the West began.

Despite the war, Mexico and California could not do without one another.

Many Mexicans have immigrated to California. The two countries are tied together economically by treaty and proximity. Many Mexicans work in California. Many have become

 The slab is from the Berlin Wall. Many Republicans credit Reagan and his policies with the collapse of the Soviet Empire as symbolized by the destruction of the Berlin Wall.

citizens or permanent residents. Hispanic culture, in architecture, cuisine, place names and radio and television shows, permeates California. The real losers were the Native Americans. Historians estimate that possibly 360,000 lived in California before the Hispanic-Anglo take over. Disease, persecution and general mistreatment reduced their numbers to about 15,000 by the early 20th century.

Only in recent decades have the injustices and cruelty been acknowledged and some attempt at reparations been made. In the 1990s, the Native Americans discovered gambling and now run some of the biggest casinos in the state.

Historical Highlights

1770s. Missionaries arrive, led by the energetic Father Junipero Serra. They start building missions and trying to domesticate Indians. Many die from diseases.

1812. Russians establish fort along Northern California coast, raising concerns that Russian may colonize state. Fears prove unfounded. Russians depart in 1841.

1821. Mexico declares its independence and takes control of California. But the Californios, used to making their own decisions, often defy governors sent from Mexico.

1820s to 1840s. California is divided into large land grants, some of which remain fairly intact to this day. Expeditions are sent into the interior to subdue the Indians. Cattle ranching dominates the economy and boosts trade with other nations, including U.S. Yankee mountain men venture into the state. In the 1840s, Yankee settlers arrive.

1844. John C. Fremont leads U.S. Army force into California. Although small, the expedition signaled a more aggressive policy toward California. The U.S. apparently feared an English takeover (down from Canada) more than Mexican intervention.

What violent event catapulted U.S. Senator Dianne Feinstein into national prominence? (Answer next page).

1846-1848. War with Mexico, mainly over Texas but tying in all Southwest. California sees a few skirmishes. At war's end, Mexico cedes California.

1848. Gold discovered at Sutter's Mill in the Sierra. Mad rush to gold fields.

1850. California becomes a state. Population hits 92,597.

1853. With several years, population booms to about 255,000. Blue jeans are first made, leading to start of Levi-Strauss and diversification of economy.

1863. Works begins on a transcontinental railroad; completed in 1869. In California, much of the work was done by Chinese immigrants, who later turned to farming. This era also sees violence against Chinese, and later Japanese, stemming in part from fears they were undercutting wages.

1860s to 1900. Railroads extended through state. Gold mining fades, farming and manufacturing picks up. State divided into counties. Literary stars: Mark Twain and Bret Harte. People start coming to California for its weather.

1868. University of California charted, Berkeley, the first campus, opened in 1873. Other campuses, notably UCLA, followed, creating the world-class UC system.

1880. University of Southern California founded in Los Angeles, the largest private university in the state.

1885. Leland Stanford, railroad magnate, and wife Jane found university. Stanford University later becomes the intellectual force behind Silicon Valley.

1900. California greets 20th century with 1,485,053 residents.

A *She was chair of the San Francisco Board of Supervisors when Mayor George Moscone and Supervisor Harvey Milk were assassinated in 1978 by a disgruntled former supervisor. Feinstein replaced Moscone as mayor and later ran successfully for the U.S. Senate.*

1905. Yosemite added to National Parks.

1906. Earthquake and fires level San Francisco — Nature shows its violent side. As other earthquakes follow, California tightens its building codes.

1907. Great Fleet arrives at San Diego harbor, further establishing U.S. as a Pacific power.

1908. First movie made in Hollywood, "The Count of Monte Christo."

1910-1991. With Hiram Johnson as governor, state adopts initiative and referendum, a form of governing that becomes popular later in the century.

1914. Panama Canal opens Asia trade making Los Angeles a port city.

1916-1918 World War I and aftermath spur California economy. 1918 Los Angeles aqueduct built. It taps water from the Owens Valley. In following decades, other projects draw water from Colorado River and Northern California rivers.

1920. Population reaches 3,426,861.

1928. Herbert Hoover, a member of the first Stanford class, is elected president.

1929 Great Depression starts. Oklahoma residents are denied entry into the state. Decade of social upheaval. John Steinbeck writes of the plight of the poor — "Grapes of Wrath."

1936. Golden Gate Bridge opens.

1940. Population 6,907,387

1941. Pearl Harbor blasts U.S. into World War II. Millions of troops are sent to California. Economy booms, bringing in workers from around the country.

Herbert Hoover

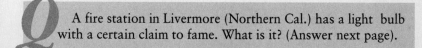

Q A fire station in Livermore (Northern Cal.) has a light bulb with a certain claim to fame. What is it? (Answer next page).

1942. Japanese residents removed to internment camps.

1942 to 1945. UC Berkeley helps build first atomic bombs.

1945-50. California economy and population surges with defense spending and veterans moving in to state.

1947. Col. Chuck Yeager breaks sound barrier at Edwards AFB in Los Angeles County.

Nixon

1950. Population breaks 10 million — 10,586,223. Over the next 50 years, California will add about 23 million people.

1950. Richard Nixon elected U.S. Senator and, in 1953, Vice President.

1950s. Jack Kerouac writes "On the Road," Dave Brubeck, "Take Five." California becomes cool.

1955. Disneyland opens in Orange County. **1958.** Dodgers quit Brooklyn, Giants leave Manhattan. Major-league baseball comes to California.

1960s. Vietnam War. Youths rebel. Free speech, Black Panthers, drugs, sex and rock and roll. California leads the way. Watts riots call attention to Black poverty. Cesar Chavez forms United Farm Workers. Robert Kennedy assassinated in Los Angeles. Ronald Reagan elected governor.

1969. Richard Nixon elected president; forced to resign in 1974 after Watergate breakin.

1970s. Tax revolt; Prop. 13 forces sweeping changes in tax code. Symbionese Liberation Army shoots Oakland schools superintendent and kidnaps Patty Hearst.

1980. Population 23,760,021.

1980s. California opens doors to immigrants, changing

A *The 4-watter has been burning steadily for over 100 years. During that time, its story has appeared in print everywhere from the local press to the National Enquirer and the Sunday Times of London and has appeared on all the major TV networks.*

ethnic makeup of state. Ronald Reagan moves into the White House.

1990. Population 29,760,021

1990s. Soviet Union goes belly up. Military shuts bases in California. Defense industries slump. About 1996, high tech starts to take off and within a few years, dotcoms send the economy rocketing. Rodney King riot in Los Angeles. Fires destroy homes in Oakland and in Los Angeles and Orange counties.

2000. New milennium. California counts 33,871,648 residents.

2001. Silicon Valley and dotcoms flop, dragging down state economy. Power crunch also hurts economy.

2002-3. Deficit blues; recall election to oust Governor Gray Davis, state runs short of money. Iraq war underscores importance of San Diego, home to many Navy ships.

Q What is the Golden Gate and who named it? (Answer next page).

Voter Registration by County

County	Dem.	Rep.	Green	Lib.	No Party
Alameda	372,317	130,393	15,977	3,409	123,806
Alpine	281	309	9	5	177
Amador	7,192	8,525	155	123	1,971
Butte	39,122	47,173	2,649	807	16,499
Calaveras	8,891	11,105	314	360	3,078
Colusa	2,917	3,419	21	33	827
Contra Costa	231,414	151,491	4,623	2,264	67,413
Del Norte	4,614	4,631	126	82	1,936
El Dorado	29,760	43,098	1,013	654	12,917
Fresno	147,039	151,781	1,713	1,331	34,642
Glenn	3,971	5,320	36	35	1,403
Humboldt	32,304	22,149	5,127	702	11,534
Imperial	27,331	14,199	131	178	7,062
Inyo	3,280	4,759	95	59	1,245
Kern	98,179	125,895	700	1,341	27,481
Kings	18,928	20,955	90	131	4,260
Lake	14,135	10,401	507	231	4,450
Lassen	4,790	6,357	66	102	2,456
Los Angeles	2,029,716	1,077,473	26,920	19,951	595,949
Madera	15,785	21,331	200	199	4,052
Marin	69,608	36,253	4,269	799	24,573
Mariposa	3,838	5,442	175	96	1,365
Mendocino	21,074	12,577	2,721	381	7,422
Merced	46,335	39,138	288	263	7,601
Modoc	1,797	2,482	25	42	626
Mono	1,760	2,440	119	65	1,098
Monterey	73,753	51,083	1,535	758	21,914
Napa	29,012	21,428	826	359	8,622
Nevada	18,514	26,924	1,877	515	9,129
Orange	414,010	635,425	6,938	9,360	199,221
Placer	46,101	79,141	1,171	955	21,156

A The Golden Gate is the entrance to San Francisco Bay. John C. Fremont, the famous explorer of early California, coined the name, long before the bridge was built. The bridge, which is painted orange, not gold, took its name from the entrance.

Voter Registration by County

County	Dem.	Rep.	Green	Lib.	No Party
Plumas	4,561	5,574	106	71	1,910
Riverside	231,374	314,641	2,585	3,569	78,189
Sacramento	260,811	209,951	5,520	2,996	82,355
San Benito	11,288	8,609	144	160	3,441
San Bernardino	246,903	256,167	2,349	3,044	72,956
San Diego	498,341	577,833	11,137	11,225	251,214
San Francisco	239,277	56,734	13,386	2,707	110,339
San Joaquin	106,012	104,818	856	834	19,390
San Luis Obispo	48,971	62,063	2,634	1,068	20,825
San Mateo	166,927	89,040	3,984	1,832	62,460
Santa Barbara	78,230	73,177	3,894	1,295	31,767
Santa Clara	337,192	218,714	6,577	5,335	149,264
Santa Cruz	69,367	31,092	6,756	1,387	22,165
Shasta	27,675	40,932	466	598	11,119
Sierra	756	963	25	32	405
Siskiyou	9,517	10,645	270	291	3,694
Solano	86,312	51,572	1,053	766	27,280
Sonoma	116,383	66,382	7,344	1,607	33,453
Stanislaus	95,949	88,511	655	765	19,415
Sutter	12,778	18,905	124	188	3,188
Tehama	10,034	11,942	110	215	3,270
Trinity	2,910	3,149	145	99	995
Tulare	46,675	60,497	456	504	13,854
Tuolumne	11,821	13,254	326	188	3,613
Ventura	149,703	160,327	3,553	2,434	56,141
Yolo	37,118	22,731	1,770	392	12,461
Yuba	9,205	10,654	162	164	3,391
State Totals	6,733,858	5,341,974	156,803	89,356	2,324,439

Source: California Secretary of State, Report of Registration 2003

What was the Pony Express and what put an end to it? (Answer next page).

Presidential Votes 1900 to Present
How California Voted

Years	Elected	%	Opponent	%
1900	William McKinley (R)	55	William Jennings Bryan (D)	41
1904	Theodore Roosevelt (R)	62	Alton Parker (D)	27
1908	William Howard Taft (R)	56	William Jennings Bryan (D)	33
1912	Woodrow Wilson (D)	42	Theodore Roosevelt (Prog.)	42
1916	Woodrow Wilson (D)	47	Charles Hughes (R)	46
1920	Warren G. Harding (R)	66	James Cox (D)	25
1924	Calvin Coolidge (R)	57	Robert Lafollette (D)	33
1928	Herbert Hoover (R)	64	Alfred Smith (D)	34
1932	Franklin D. Roosevelt (D)	58	Herbert Hoover (R)	37
1936	Franklin D. Roosevelt (D)	67	Alfred Landon (R)	32
1940	Franklin D. Roosevelt (D)	57	Wendell Willkie (R)	41
1944	Franklin D. Roosevelt (D)	57	Thomas Dewey (R)	47
1948	Harry Truman (D)	48	Thomas Dewey (R)	47
1952	Dwight Eisenhower (R)	56	Adlai Stevenson (D)	43
1956	Dwight Eisenhower (R)	55	Adlai Stevenson (D)	44
1960	John F. Kennedy (D)	50	Richard Nixon (R)	50
1964	Lyndon Johnson (D)	59	Barry Goldwater (R)	41
1968	Richard Nixon (R)	48	Hubert Humphrey (D)	45
1972	Richard Nixon (R)	55	George McGovern (D)	42
1976	Jimmy Carter (D)	48	Gerald Ford (R)	50
1980	Ronald Reagan (R)	53	Jimmy Carter (D)	36
1984	Ronald Reagan (R)	58	Walter Mondale (D)	41
1988	George Bush (R)	51	Michael Dukakis (D)	48
1992	Bill Clinton (D)	46	George Bush (R)	33
1996	Bill Clinton (D)	51	Bob Dole (R)	38
2000	George W. Bush (R)	42	Al Gore (D)	54

Source: California Secretary of State

In the 1850's, California was isolated from the rest of the country. To speed mail delivery, the Pony Express was started in 1860. In relays, teenagers and young men galloped horses from St. Joseph, Missouri, to Sacramento, 1,966 miles. On October 24, 1861, a transcontinental telegraph linked West with East, instant messaging. Two days later, the Pony Express folded.

County Vote Results
Gore, Bush, Nader

Counties	Gore DEM	Bush REP	Nader GRN
Alameda	342,889	119,279	27,499
Alpine	265	281	25
Amador	5,906	8,766	584
Butte	31,338	45,584	5,727
Calaveras	7,093	10,599	863
Colusa	1,745	3,629	151
Contra Costa	224,338	141,373	13,067
Del Norte	3,117	4,526	485
El Dorado	26,220	42,045	3,013
Fresno	95,059	117,342	6,541
Glenn	2,498	5,795	268
Humboldt	24,851	23,219	7,100
Imperial	15,489	12,524	608
Inyo	2,652	4,713	344
Kern	66,003	110,663	3,474
Kings	11,041	16,377	567
Lake	10,717	8,699	1,265
Lassen	2,982	7,080	339
Los Angeles	1,710,505	871,930	83,731
Madera	11,650	20,283	1,080
Marin	79,135	34,872	8,289
Mariposa	2,816	4,727	379
Mendocino	16,634	12,272	5,051
Merced	22,726	26,102	1,166
Modoc	945	2,969	122
Mono	1,788	2,296	230
Monterey	67,618	43,761	5,059
Napa	28,097	20,633	2,471
Nevada	17,670	25,998	3,287
Orange	391,819	541,299	26,833

 What famous soap associated with Ronald Reagan came from the California desert? (Answer next page).

County Vote Results

Counties	Gore DEM	Bush REP	Nader GRN
Placer	42,449	69,835	4,449
Plumas	3,458	6,343	456
Riverside	202,576	231,955	11,678
Sacramento	212,792	195,619	17,659
San Benito	9,131	7,015	535
San Bernardino	214,749	221,757	11,775
San Diego	437,666	475,736	33,979
San Francisco	241,578	51,496	24,828
San Joaquin	79,776	81,773	4,195
San Luis Obispo	44,526	56,859	6,523
San Mateo	166,757	80,296	10,433
Santa Barbara	73,411	71,493	8,664
Santa Clara	332,490	188,750	19,072
Santa Cruz	66,618	29,627	10,844
Shasta	20,127	43,278	2,131
Sierra	540	1,172	86
Siskiyou	6,323	12,198	872
Solano	75,116	51,604	3,869
Sonoma	117,295	63,529	14,324
Stanislaus	56,448	67,188	3,398
Sutter	8,416	17,350	594
Tehama	6,507	13,270	697
Trinity	1,932	3,340	396
Tulare	33,006	54,070	1,834
Tuolumne	9,359	13,172	949
Ventura	133,258	136,173	10,235
Yolo	33,747	23,057	4,107
Yuba	5,546	9,838	507
State Total	5,861,203	4,567,429	418,707

Source: California Secretary of State

A 20-Mule Team Borax and Boraxo, *made from Borax mined in Death Valley, were for decades among the most popular soaps in the U.S. The borax was hauled from mines and carted out of the desert in giant wagons, each pulled by 20 mules. Reagan hosted a low-budget T.V. western show, Death Valley Days, sponsored by the makers of 20-Mule Team Borax.*

5

Crime

California crime peaked in 1980, dropped slowly in the 1980s, then sharply in the 1990s. In 1980, the state recorded 3,405 homicides; in 2002, the count was 2,392.

In the 1980s, new laws locked up more offenders. Between 1980 and 2000, state prisoners went from 23,000 to 161,000.

With the budget crunch, policies may be revised to release more nonviolent prisoners and cut costs but, leery of crime, voters do not seem inclined to make sweeping changes. Homicides have been inching up the last few years. Here are 2001 and 2002 statistics from the California Dept. of Justice.

- Between 2001 and 2002, the number of assaults dropped but homicides, rapes and property crimes showed increases.

- In 2002, about 1,426,000 adults were arrested, an increase of 6,000 over 2001. In the same period, about 229,600 juveniles were arrested, a drop of 11,000.

- Firearms continue to be the weapon of choice in California killings, 72 percent of all homicides and 85 percent of victims aged 18-29 (2001 data).

- In 2002, California's death row population stood at 610. Of these, 25 were sentenced in 2001.

- Six police officers were slain in 2001; sixty-three since 1992.

Who was the "Red Light Bandit" and why did he cause so much political anguish? (Answer on next page).

Crime By State

States	Population	Rate	Homicides
Alabama	4,464,356	43	379
Alaska	634,892	42	39
Arizona	5,307,331	61	400
Arkansas	2,692,090	41	148
California	34,501,130	39	2,206
Colorado	4,417,714	42	158
Connecticut	3,425,074	31	105
Delaware	796,165	41	23
Florida	16,396,515	56	874
Georgia	8,383,915	46	598
Hawaii	1,224,398	54	32
Idaho	1,321,006	31	30
Illinois	12,482,301	41	986
Indiana	6,114,745	38	413
Iowa	2,923,179	33	50
Kansas	2,694,641	43	92
Kentucky	4,065,556	29	191
Louisiana	4,465,430	53	501
Maine	1,286,670	27	18
Maryland	5,375,156	49	446
Massachusetts	6,379,304	31	145
Michigan	9,990,817	41	672
Minnesota	4,972,294	36	119
Mississippi	2,858,029	42	282
Missouri	5,629,707	48	372
Montana	904,433	37	34
Nebraska	1,713,235	43	43

A Caryl Chessman, who had a high I.Q., was known as the redlight bandit because he used a red light to pull over unsuspecting women and later assault them. Sentenced to death, he became a symbol of opposition to the death penalty. He won several delays and then was executed in 1960.

Crime By State

States	Population	Rate	Homicides
Nevada	2,106,074	43	180
New Hampshire	1,259,181	23	17
New Jersey	8,484,431	32	336
New Mexico	1,829,146	53	99
New York	19,011,378	29	*960
North Carolina	8,186,268	49	505
North Dakota	634,448	24	7
Ohio	11,373,541	42	452
Oklahoma	3,460,097	46	185
Oregon	3,472,867	50	84
Pennsylvania	12,287,150	30	651
Rhode Island	1,058,920	37	39
South Carolina	4,063,011	48	255
South Dakota	756,600	23	7
Tennessee	5,740,021	52	425
Texas	21,325,018	52	1,332
Utah	2,269,789	42	67
Vermont	613,090	28	7
Virginia	7,187,734	32	364
Washington	5,987,973	52	179
West Virginia	1,801,916	26	40
Wisconsin	5,401,906	33	192
Wyoming	494,423	35	9
Washington D.C.	571,822	77	232

Source: FBI Index of Crime by State 2001. Rate is all reported willful homicides, rapes, aggravated assaults, burglaries, motor vehicle thefts, larceny thefts and arsons per 1,000 residents. Homicides include murders and manslaughters.

*The 2,823 people killed on Sept. 11 at the World Trade Center are not included here.

During the 1920s, gangsters captured the residents of this small farm town and then let them loose. Where and why? (Answer next page).

Crime by County

Counties	Population	Rate	Homicides
Alameda	1,496,200	23	144
Alpine	1,210	27	0
Amador	36,500	16	0
Butte	210,400	17	5
Calaveras	42,450	16	2
Colusa	19,700	13	0
Contra Costa	994,900	19	48
Del Norte	27,850	20	2
El Dorado	166,000	13	4
Fresno	841,400	27	62
Glenn	27,050	12	0
Humboldt	128,300	16	12
Imperial	150,900	21	3
Inyo	18,350	9	0
Kern	702,900	19	51
Kings	136,100	13	4
Lake	61,300	19	4
Lassen	34,950	7	0
Los Angeles	9,979,600	22	1,162
Madera	131,200	20	6
Marin	250,400	10	4
Mariposa	17,450	13	0
Mendocino	88,200	16	4
Merced	225,100	24	18
Modoc	9,325	13	0
Mono	13,350	13	0
Monterey	415,800	14	28
Napa	129,800	10	2
Nevada	95,700	10	3
Orange	2,978,800	11	77
Placer	275,600	11	0

A Pescadero, located just south of San Francisco. During the prohibition era when alcohol was outlawed, bootleggers smuggled in a shipment and buried it near Pescadero. Some enterprising locals dug it up, which greatly irritated the smugglers. They invaded the town, manhandled a few residents, got their booze back and departed.

Crime by County

Counties	Population	Rate	Homicides
Plumas	20,900	15	0
Riverside	1,705,500	21	111
Sacramento	1,309,600	25	83
San Benito	56,300	12	1
San Bernardino	1,833,000	21	141
San Diego	2,961,600	18	87
San Francisco	791,600	23	68
San Joaquin	613,500	29	59
San Luis Obispo	256,300	11	3
San Mateo	717,000	10	21
Santa Barbara	410,300	9	8
Santa Clara	1,729,900	10	37
Santa Cruz	259,800	13	6
Shasta	172,000	17	5
Sierra	3,520	7	0
Siskiyou	44,400	9	4
Solano	412,000	18	16
Sonoma	472,700	13	16
Stanislaus	481,600	24	15
Sutter	83,200	17	7
Tehama	57,700	14	2
Trinity	13,300	12	0
Tulare	386,200	24	29
Tuolumne	56,500	17	2
Ventura	791,300	9	21
Yolo	181,300	18	5
Yuba	62,800	26	0
California	35,591,000	6	2,392

Source: California Dept. of Justice, 2002 data. Crime rate is based on major crimes per 1,000 residents.

Q What Contra Costa County housekeeper turned out to be a notorious murderess? (Answer next page).

40 Safest Cities In U.S. (Population over 100,000)

Rank	City / State	Population	Crime	Rate	Homicides
1	Simi Valley, California	113,420	1,746	15	6
2	Thousand Oaks, California	119,179	1,888	16	1
3	Amherst Town, New York	111,169	2,010	18	0
4	Sunnyvale, California	134,209	2,698	20	0
5	Santa Clarita, California	153,896	3,161	21	3
6	Daly City, California	105,547	2,300	22	5
7	Glendale, California	198,596	4,491	23	5
8	Huntington Beach, California	193,117	4,500	23	0
9	Irvine, California	145,731	3,396	23	0
10	Stamford, Connecticut	117,754	3,086	26	1
11	Orange, California	131,215	3,692	28	0
12	San Jose, California	913,513	25,163	28	22
13	Sterling Heights, Michigan	125,127	3,552	28	0
14	Yonkers, New York	196,447	5,419	28	6
15	Rancho Cucamonga, California	130,117	3,805	29	1
16	Fontana, California	131,325	3,969	30	10
17	Fremont, California	207,193	6,152	30	0
18	Oxnard, California	173,524	5,250	30	6
19	Coral Springs, Florida	120,595	3,604	30	2
20	Garden Grove, California	168,266	5,176	31	5

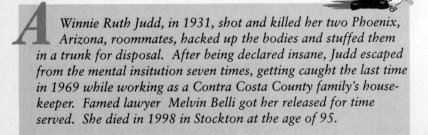

A Winnie Ruth Judd, in 1931, shot and killed her two Phoenix, Arizona, roommates, hacked up the bodies and stuffed them in a trunk for disposal. After being declared insane, Judd escaped from the mental insitution seven times, getting caught the last time in 1969 while working as a Contra Costa County family's house-keeper. Famed lawyer Melvin Belli got her released for time served. She died in 1998 in Stockton at the age of 95.

40 Safest Cities In U.S. (Population over 100,000)

Rank	City / State	Population	Crime	Rate	Homicides
21	Torrance, California	140,510	4,366	31	4
22	Livonia, Michigan	101,075	3,113	31	1
23	Henderson, Nevada	184,844	5,728	31	9
24	El Monte, California	118,120	3,778	32	10
25	Santa Clara, California	104,263	3,350	32	0
26	Manchester, New Hampshire	109,032	3,520	32	0
27	Burbank, California	102,180	3,377	33	3
28	Corona, California	127,288	4,218	33	3
29	Ventura, California	102,791	3,357	33	2
30	New York, New York	8,023,018	266,587	33	3,472
31	Sioux Falls, South Dakota	124,263	4,130	33	2
32	Anaheim, California	334,110	11,225	34	8
33	Downey, California	109,318	3,715	34	5
34	Ann Arbor, Michigan	114,625	3,880	34	1
35	Carrollton, Texas	112,063	3,842	34	2
36	Norwalk, California	105,218	3,656	35	7
37	Santa Ana, California	344,258	12,066	35	24
38	Cape Coral, Florida	104,936	3,670	35	2
39	Costa Mesa, California	110,745	4,021	36	4
40	Fullerton, California	128,345	4,555	36	3

Source: FBI, 2001 data. Crime rate is based on major crimes per 1,000 residents.

 What son of a famous singer/actor was abducted in 1963? (Answer next page).

Crime in Other Cities Nationwide

City	Population	Rate	Homicides
Anchorage	263,588	50	10
Atlanta	426,511	123	144
Birmingham	243,762	86	73
Boise	189,671	46	2
Boston	591,944	63	65
Chicago	2,866,191	NA	628
Cleveland	479,263	69	77
Dallas	1,215,553	91	240
Denver	569,653	53	45
Des Moines	198,468	64	11
Hartford, Conn	122,274	88	25
Detroit, MI	956,283	94	395
Honolulu	885,605	55	20
Jacksonville	754,679	68	75
Las Vegas	1,117,763	45	133
Little Rock	184,413	91	34
Milwaukee	601,229	76	127
Miami	371,863	95	66
New York City	8,023,018	33	*3,472
New Orleans	484,289	75	213
Oklahoma City	507,517	90	45
Pittsburgh, PA	331,414	58	55
Phoenix	1,366,542	77	209
Portland, OR	537,081	80	21
Reno	190,218	58	6
St. Louis, MO	350,336	150	148
Salt Lake City	184,723	89	18
Scottsdale, AZ	209,686	47	10
Seattle	572,345	81	25
Tucson	503,461	99	42

Source: Annual 2002 FBI crime report, which uses 2001 data. Population estimates are based on updated estimates from 2000 census. Key: NA (not available).

*Note: New York City's homicides includes 2,823 people killed on Sept. 11, 2001 at World Trade Center.

 Frank Sinatra Jr., then 19, was kidnapped on Dec. 8, 1963, from a Lake Tahoe casino by two men who later released him for ransom. They didn't get to spend much of it because they were quickly caught and convicted.

Crime In California's Cities

City	Population	Rate	Homicides
Anaheim	337,400	36	18
Bakersfield	266,800	44	22
Berkeley	104,600	99	7
Burbank	104,500	33	1
Chula Vista	199,700	38	5
Concord	124,900	45	3
Corona	137,000	33	8
Costa Mesa	111,500	34	2
Daly City	104,300	21	2
Downey	111,700	33	1
El Monte	121,900	30	7
Escondido	138,000	40	4
Fontana	145,800	30	7
Fremont	209,000	27	3
Fresno	448,500	77	42
Fullerton	131,500	37	1
Garden Grove	169,900	32	6
Glendale	202,700	23	9
Hayward	144,700	39	9
Huntington Beach	197,000	22	3
Inglewood	117,000	35	28
Irvine	164,900	22	1
Long Beach	481,000	41	67
Los Angeles	3,864,400	50	653
Modesto	203,300	64	5
Oakland	412,200	73	108
Oceanside	169,800	41	5

 In 1980, a Northern California teenager was struck and killed by a car. This led her mother to co-found what organization? (Answer next page).

Crime In California's Cities

City	Population	Rate	Homicides
Ontario	165,700	51	7
Orange	134,500	29	1
Oxnard	181,800	30	10
Pasadena	142,200	35	3
Pomona	156,500	39	18
Richmond	101,400	78	29
Riverside	274,100	56	23
Sacramento	433,400	72	47
Salinas	150,300	46	20
San Bernardino	194,100	71	42
San Diego	1,275,100	39	47
San Francisco	791,600	54	62
San Jose	925,000	26	28
Santa Ana	347,200	35	23
Santa Clara	105,800	31	4
Santa Rosa	154,500	43	6
Simi Valley	117,700	15	0
Stockton	261,300	81	36
Sunnyvale	132,500	20	2
Torrance	144,400	32	1
Vallejo	120,100	60	7
Ventura	104,300	35	2
West Covina	110,500	39	2

Source: California Dept. of Justice, 2002 data

A Candi Lightner formed Mothers Against Drunk Driving
(MADD) after a drunken driver slammed into her 13-year-
old daughter, Cari, as she was walking to school in Fair Oaks.
After learning that her daughter's killer had a previous history
of drunken driving, Lightner met at a Sacramento steakhouse
with friends and a Maryland mother whose daughter had been
crippled by a repeat drunken driver and formed MADD.

U.S. Crime

- In 2001, the FBI reports, 13,752 people were murdered in the United States. Of these, 8,719 or 63 percent were shot, 1,796 stabbed, 661 beaten with blunt instrument, 925 as saulted with feet, hands or fists, 10 poisoned, 104 killed by fire, 23 drowned and 152 strangled. Narcotics killed 34 and asphyxiation 112. In 1,212 homicides, weapons were not identified. (These numbers and the following do not include the 2,893 people lost on Sept. 11, 2001 at World Trade Center)
- Of total murdered, 10,503 were male, 3,214 female and 35 unknown.
- In murders involving guns, handguns accounted for 6,790 deaths, rifles 389, shotguns 497 and other guns or type unknown 1,043.
- Of the 13,572 murdered in 2001, the FBI reported that 4,007 lost their lives in violence stemming from arguments or brawls. The next largest category was robbery victims, 1,042 homicides. Romantic triangles led to 118 homicides, narcotics 558, juvenile gang violence 865, gangland violence 74, rape 59, arson 70, baby-sitter-killing-child 37, burglary 73, prostitution 5, gambling 3.
- In 2001, there were 585 justifiable homicides in the U.S. — 370 by police officers, 215 by private citizens.
- In 1995, the U.S. recorded 20,232 homicides. In 1996, the number took a big drop, 16,967. The following year they decreased to 15,837 and the next year to 14,276. In 1999, the FBI tallied 13,011 homicides and in 2000, the amount shrunk again, to 12,943. Among possible reasons for decline: better emergency-trauma care, locking up more people, prosperity, more cops. Although 2001 homicides, minus the September 11 deaths, showed an increase, they are still well below the 1995 figures — 13,752 vs. 20,232.

What Sacramento landlady's crimes resembled a scene right out of "Arsenic and Old Lace?" (Answer next page).

California Prisoner Population

Year	Male	Females	Total
1993	108,302	7,232	115,534
1994	116,879	7,934	124,813
1995	122,514	8,828	131,342
1996	131,273	9,744	141,017
1997	141,669	10,837	152,506
1998	147,001	11,206	158,207
1999	150,581	11,483	162,064
2000	150,793	11,207	162,000
2001	150,785	10,712	161,497
2002	148,153	9,826	157,979
2003	150,629	9,903	160,532
2004	151,318	9,969	161,287

Source: California Dept. of Corrections (Projections for 2003/2004)

California Crime

Of the 2,201 homicides committed in 2001, guns accounted for 1,568 deaths, or 72 percent of the total, knives 298, blunt objects such as clubs 95, hands and feet other personal weapons 103, and unidentified weapons 110. (Cal. Dept. of Justice).

A Dorothea Puente was arrested in 1989, accused of poisoning nine tenants at her Sacramento boarding house, seven of whom were found buried in the yard. After poisoning and burying her "guests," Puente cashed their pension checks. She was convicted of killing three victims and was imprisoned.

Downright Bad

Here are some of the notorious criminals who have shocked Californians in recent decades.

Charles Manson

A cult leader whose charismatic powers led followers to murder, Charles Manson was involved in the Aug. 9, 1969 killings of actress Sharon Tate, her unborn baby and her guests Abigail Folger, Voytek Frykowski, and Jay Sebring. Ms. Tate was married to Roman Polanski, who in 2003 won an Oscar for directing "The Pianist." The next day businessman Leno LaBianca and wife Rosemary joined the list of Manson-family victims. Manson followers murdered three other people, including their own defense attorney, Ronald Hughes. Now serving a life term, Manson retains his cult status. Fans have created numerous websites devoted to him and his music. He has received more mail than any other U.S. inmate, and has repeatedly caused trouble to the prison authorities. He has been denied parole repeatedly.

Manson Family Killers

Patricia Krenwinkel, Leslie Van Houten and Susan Atkins were all devoted members of the Manson "Family." Along with Manson, they were convicted of the seven Tate-LaBianca murders and are at a California institution for women. Atkins has married twice while in prison, and Van Houten is a model prisoner whose case for parole has aroused sympathy. Her lawyer argues that substantial intake of LSD had altered her brain at the time of the killings.

How did early San Franciscans cope with lawlessness and crime? (Answer next page).

Squeaky Fromme

Convicted for the attempted assassination of President Gerald Ford in 1975, former Manson family member Lynette "Squeaky" Fromme was sentenced to life in prison. In addition to her present cell home, she also has been housed in a prison in San Diego, the Federal Correctional Institution in Dublin (from which she briefly escaped), a maximum-security prison in Lexington, Kentucky, and a maximum security unit at Marianna, Florida.

The Menendez Brothers

Lyle and Erik Menendez are the sons of a successful and wealthy Cuban-American business executive, Jose Menendez. In 1989, as the brothers reached college age, they had grown resentful of the demands placed on them by their parents. Wanting to cash in on the family millions and rid themselves of parental discipline, the pair shotgunned their mother and father, killing them. After two highly publicized trials, they were convicted of first-degree murder in 1996, and each received two consecutive life prison terms without the possibility of parole.

Sirhan Sirhan

In the summer of 1965, Sirhan Sirhan shot to death Robert Kennedy in a Los Angeles hotel, believing him to be anti-Arab. Kennedy, the brother of President John F. Kennedy, was running for president. Sirhan was apprehended on the scene, and subsequently convicted. He is serving a life sentence and so far has been denied parole 12 times. At trial, Sirhan said that he killed Kennedy "premeditatedly with 20 years of malice aforethought." He subsequently apologized for the killing, and now says he remembers nothing about the shooting.

In 1851, they formed a "vigilance" committee run by merchants and sea captains. During its four-month reign, the committee was responsible for 90 arrests, four hangings, one whipping and 28 deportations.

Sara Jane Moore

Sara Jane Moore was imprisoned for attempting to assassinate President Gerald Ford in San Francisco in 1975. In February 5, 1979, while incarcerated for the crime, the former resident of Contra Costa County escaped, but was recaptured the following day. She appeared calm on April 6, 1979, when a jury found her guilty of escaping from prison. But in her testimony the day before, she had sobbed that she fled to keep her sanity. Moore said "There's nothing about being a prisoner that says you can't remain a human being, and they won't let you."

Charles Ng

In 1984-85, Leonard Lake and Charles Ng kidnapped victims of both sexes and varying ages, and took them to a remote site in Calaveras County where they tortured, raped and murdered them. Lake, upon being caught, swallowed a poison pill and died almost instantaneously. Ng escaped to Canada where he avoided trial for several years. Once back in California, Ng appeared before six different judges in a case that amassed over six tons of evidence and documents costing nearly $10 million. Following 13 years of delays, Ng went to trial in October 1998, and after eight months, with minimal deliberation, the jury returned a guilty verdict for the murders of six men, three women and two baby boys. Sentenced to death, Ng is employing all available appeals.

Angelo Buono and Kenneth Bianchi

In a short period between 1977 and 1978, Los Angeles police found the naked bodies of 10 women who had been raped and murdered. The victims were left on hillsides and other locations where they would be found. The media dubbed the killer "The Hillside Strangler," but, as it turned out, two cousins—Kenneth

 Which pillar of Marin society made no attempts to hide the fact that in the 1930s and 1940s she was the madam of a San Francisco bordello? (Answer next page).

Bianchi and Angelo Buono—were implicated. Bianchi had moved to Los Angeles to live with his cousin Angelo Buono and he quickly adopted the older man's perversities. Buono and Bianchi, posing as patrolmen, pulled over women at night, then kidnapped, tortured, raped and killed them. Within four months, the pair victimized 10 girls and women, ages 12 to 28. Bianchi then moved to Washington where he raped and murdered a former co-worker and her girlfriend—but this time he got caught. He pled guilty and, in exchange for no death penalty, testified against Buono. The Los Angeles trial lasted two years. Bianchi pled guilty to five of the murders and Buono was found guilty of nine out of ten. Both were sentenced to life. Buono died in prison in 2002, and Bianchi is still behind bars.

"Stars" Behind Bars

Here are nine of California's most celebrated bad guys and gals. See if you can match the jailbirds to the jail in which they're incarcerated.

Kenneth Bianchi	Alderson, W. Virginia
Squeaky Fromme	Carswell, Texas
Charles Ng	Corcoran, CA (Central Valley)
Charles Manson	Folsom, CA
Manson Family	Frontera, Chino, CA
Erik Menendez	San Quentin, CA
Lyle Menendez	Tehachapi, (east of Bakersfield)
Sara Jane Moore	Walla Walla, Washington
Sirhan Sirhan	

Answers: Bianchi-Walla Walla; Fromme-Carswell; Ng-San Quentin; Manson-Corcoran; Manson Family Killers-Frontera; Erik Menendez-Folsom; Lyle Menendez-Tehachapi; Moore-Alderson; Sirhan-Corcoran

When Sally Stanford successfully ran for mayor of Sausalito in 1972, voters disregarded her notorious past, figuring she had common sense.

6

Transit

California has sworn off freeways — sort of.

The newest and maybe the last freeway for some time, Highway 210, is under construction in San Bernardino County.

Meanwhile throughout the state, freeways are being upgraded with new overpasses, diamond lanes and other improvements.

Three new bridges are going up in the Bay Area, two of them replacing existing bridges.

Over the last 20 years, trains and light rail have gotten a good boost.

Los Angeles, with great difficulty, built a subway line from its downtown to Hollywood and to the San Fernando Valley. In 2003, a rail line was opened between downtown L.A. and Pasadena.

In 2003, BART (Bay Area Rapid Transit) extended its line to San Francisco International Airport.

Transit officials continue to experiment with diamond lanes and incentives to get more solo drivers into car pools.

Ferries are making a minor comeback in the Bay Area.

For the future: look to the bus. Changes are being made to make them more comfortable and faster in traffic. Diamond lanes, many of them installed over the last two decades, allow buses to whiz around traffic jams.

 How many of those highway cones does the California Dept. of Transportation buy every year: 10-15,000, 35-40,000, 60-65,000? (Answer next page.)

Drivers & Vehicles

Counties	Vehicle Registration	Motorcycle Registration	Licensed Drivers
Alameda	1,100,175	21,958	951,580
Alpine	1,525	53	977
Amador	36,927	974	25,294
Butte	160,104	3,632	140,591
Calaveras	45,727	1,339	31,663
Colusa	16,235	227	12,020
Contra Costa	755,532	15,687	655,268
Del Norte	19,041	363	16,508
El Dorado	146,992	4,161	119,665
Fresno	510,285	8,290	448,732
Glenn	22,578	391	17,514
Humboldt	107,100	2,570	91,219
Imperial	101,590	923	83,141
Inyo	19,497	557	14,426
Kern	441,834	9,104	377,865
Kings	70,904	1,340	59,768
Lake	57,934	1,387	41,705
Lassen	23,799	527	18,668
Los Angeles	6,236,732	81,167	5,542,093
Madera	81,411	1,481	66,369
Marin	218,765	5,248	188,207
Mariposa	18,591	527	13,113
Mendocino	81,132	2,010	62,296
Merced	141,225	2,267	117,254
Modoc	8,456	90	6,423
Mono	11,978	407	8,779
Monterey	282,122	4,838	233,831
Napa	106,567	2,258	86,091
Nevada	91,624	2,816	74,887
Orange	2,125,552	34,155	1,905,170
Placer	226,412	5,811	186,325

A 35,000 - 40,000.

Drivers & Vehicles

Counties	Vehicle Registration	Motorcycle Registration	Licensed Drivers
Plumas	23,160	577	16,584
Riverside	1,056,744	18,677	934,924
Sacramento	896,887	15,904	789,062
San Benito	42,444	1,438	32,806
San Bernardino	1,138,996	20,838	1,006,576
San Diego	2,122,800	39,840	1,885,027
San Francisco	451,879	16,537	514,778
San Joaquin	395,201	6,817	331,333
San Luis Obispo	207,956	5,585	172,138
San Mateo	683,017	12,010	503,230
Santa Barbara	306,464	6,964	265,539
Santa Clara	1,378,629	28,000	1,181,103
Santa Cruz	208,076	6,727	174,216
Shasta	140,924	3,334	119,835
Sierra	3,753	91	2,582
Siskiyou	44,581	941	34,481
Solano	297,951	6,600	251,749
Sonoma	401,118	9,463	323,930
Stanislaus	322,612	6,190	275,023
Sutter	61,371	1,047	51,481
Tehama	43,233	829	37,201
Trinity	13,332	389	9,694
Tulare	239,434	4,093	201,098
Tuolumne	54,065	1,668	39,275
Ventura	602,137	13,799	511,511
Yolo	121,326	2,057	104,678
Yuba	43,407	891	36,813
Statewide Total	24,714,595	450,030	21,404,109

Source: Dept. of Motor Vehicles 2000

What airport was deliberately built in one of the foggiest spots in California? (Answer next page).

Love That Car
U.S. and California Commuting

Commuting To Work	U.S. Number	U.S. Percent	California Number	California Percent
Workers*	128,279,228	100%	14,525,322	100%
Drive alone	97,102,050	76%	10,432,462	72%
Carpooled	15,634,051	12%	2,113,313	15%
Public trans. (including taxi)	6,067,703	5%	736,037	5%
Walked	3,758,982	3%	414,581	3%
Other means	1,532,219	1%	271,893	2%
Worked at home	4,184,223	3%	557,036	4%

Average minutes to work   US – 26 Minutes   CAL – 28 Minutes

Source: DP3-Economic Characteristics 2000
*16 years and over

McKinleyville. *The town's airport, still in operation as the Humboldt County Airport, was built in the 1930s by the U.S. Navy to test landings in fog.*

Accidents Related to Inattention

Inattention Reason	Fatal	Injury	Property Damage Only	Total	%
Cell Phone	6	264	341	611	11%
Electronics	0	25	46	71	1%
Radio/CD	0	226	293	519	9%
Smoking	0	24	48	72	1%
Eating	1	74	132	207	3%
Children	1	112	121	234	4%
Animals	0	23	28	51	1%
Personal Hygiene	1	13	8	22	1%
Reading	1	61	50	112	2%
Other*	20	1,572	2,186	3,778	67%
Total Parties	**30**	**2,394**	**3,253**	**5,677**	**100%**

*"Other" includes all reasons not identified in the previous categories. Examples include but are not limited to: daydreaming, visual distractions, reading street signs, and statements by drivers of general inattention.
(Numbers rounded to nearest percentage point)
Source: California Highway Patrol 2002

How many hours are wasted in freeway backups in a year? (Answer next page).

Killed or Injured — Motor Vehicles

One Year Tally by County

Counties	Killed	Injured
Alameda	114	13,266
Alpine	4	55
Amador	9	356
Butte	27	1,506
Calaveras	9	393
Colusa	3	226
Contra Costa	59	6,263
Del Norte	6	285
El Dorado	29	1,521
Fresno	126	7,222
Glenn	4	169
Humboldt	24	1,160
Imperial	55	1,172
Inyo	11	226
Kern	150	5,686
Kings	29	967
Lake	27	536
Lassen	6	299
Los Angeles	749	88,801
Madera	27	1,222
Marin	13	1,867
Mariposa	4	135
Mendocino	22	807
Merced	56	2,171
Modoc	1	99
Mono	6	179
Monterey	53	2,908
Napa	24	1,344
Nevada	14	941
Orange	164	22,996

A *The Texas Transportation Institute says in its annual Urban Mobility Report (2002) that the average rush-hour driver in the U.S. is doomed to about 62 hours in gridlock hell. In Los Angeles, that's a very good number. L.A.'s freeways gobble up 136 hours annually. That's not ordinary driving time, just time sitting and sitting and sitting and cursing.*

Killed or Injured — Motor Vehicles

One Year Tally by County

Counties	Killed	Injured
Placer	24	2,498
Plumas	12	238
Riverside	266	12,968
Sacramento	117	14,082
San Benito	19	513
San Bernardino	318	15,786
San Diego	260	23,399
San Francisco	49	6,913
San Joaquin	110	6,956
San Luis Obispo	31	1,877
San Mateo	45	5,066
Santa Barbara	32	2,816
Santa Clara	103	13,907
Santa Cruz	19	1,917
Shasta	31	1,805
Sierra	1	44
Siskiyou	15	361
Solano	37	3,401
Sonoma	46	4,391
Stanislaus	78	5,288
Sutter	21	767
Tehama	22	568
Trinity	8	166
Tulare	107	3,565
Tuolumne	7	485
Ventura	87	6,418
Yolo	23	1,375
Yuba	17	675
State Total	3,730	303,023

Source: Dept. of Motor Vehicles 2000

Q In 2003, a graceful suspension bridge was being erected over the Carquinez Strait from Crockett to Vallejo in Northern California. The bridge was named after Al Zampa, a member of the Halfway to Hell club. Who was Zampa and what was the club? (Answer next page).

Major California Bridges

Bridge	Built	Length	Toll
1. Antioch Bridge	1978	1.6 miles	$2
2. Benicia-Martinez Bridge*	1962	6,215 feet	$2
3. Carquinez Bridge	1958	.8 mile	$2
4. Carquinez Bridge**	2003-4	.8 mile	$2
5. Dumbarton Bridge	1982	8,600 feet	$2
6. Golden Gate Bridge	1939	1.7 miles	$5
7. Richmond-San Rafael Bridge	1956	5.5 miles	$2
8. San Diego-Coronado Bridge	1969	11,179 feet	none
9. San Francisco Bay Bridge	1936	8.5 miles	$2
10. San Mateo-Hayward Bridge***	1967	5.6 miles	$2
11. Vincent Thomas (San Pedro)	1963	6,060 feet	none

*Second bridge now under construction.

**Two motor-vehicle bridges span the Carquinez Strait at the entrance to the Sacramento River-Delta. The older, built in 1927, is to be demolished following the completion of a suspension bridge, now under construction.

*** The San Mateo bridge was built with extra lanes at its west end. A "second" bridge, recently built, ties into the first on the west side.

Note: all tolls collected one way.

*A*lfred Zampa was an ironworker who helped build the original Carquinez Bridge plus the Oakland-San Francisco and Golden Gate bridges. In 1936, while working on the Golden Gate, he slipped on a wet girder and fell, only to be caught by a net suspended under the bridge, end to end. This net saved the lives of 19 ironworkers, who formed themselves into the Halfway to Hell Club.

Excuses, Excuses ....

Heard by toll collectors on the Oakland-San Francisco Bay Bridge:

- *"Someone hit me over the head and took my wallet."*
- *"I spent all my money buying gas."*
- *"I left my purse/wallet at home/work (most used)."*
- *"I am broke, I just don't have it (second most)."*
- *"My wife/husband took all my money out of my wallet/purse."*
- *"My grandma is dying."*
- *"My money blew away."*
- *"This is my first time ... do I have to pay?"*
- *"I never carry cash. Will you take credit cards?"*
- *"I forgot."*
- *"I just got robbed."*
- *"I didn't know there was a bridge here."*
- *"My dog ate my money."*
- *"I just had the money. It disappeared."*
- *"I just spent all my money buying this BMW."*

Toll takers get an average 200 "no pays" a day. They will issue an emergency payment notice. If you don't pay within 5 days, you get another bill for $12 (includes $10 fine).

Word of Advice: Don't run the toll booth. Pay later.

 When Southern California news announcers want to call attention to traffic jams, they use the term "Sig-Alert." What is a Sig-Alert? (Answer next page).

Large Public Airports in California

Airport	Town	Runway Length (ft)
Castle	Atwater	11,802
Burbank-Glendale-Pasadena	Burbank	6,886
McClellan-Palomar	Carlsbad	4,897
Fresno-Yosemite Int'l.	Fresno	9,217
John Wayne International	Irvine	5,701
Long Beach	Long Beach	10,000
Los Angeles International	Los Angeles	12,091
Modesto City-County	Modesto	5,911
Mojave Airport	Mojave	9,600
Metropolitan Oakland Int'l	Oakland	10,000
Ontario International	Ontario	12,198
Palm Springs International	Palm Springs	10,000
AF Plant 42	Palmdale	12,002
Sacramento International	Sacramento	8,601
McClellan Airfield	Sacramento	10,600
Sacramento Mather	Sacramento	11,301
San Bernardino International	San Bernardino	10,001
San Diego Int'l-Lindbergh Field	San Diego	9,400
San Francisco International	San Francisco	11,870
San Jose International (Mineta)	San Jose	11,000
Santa Barbara Municipal	Santa Barbara	6,052
Santa Monica Municipal	Santa Monica	4,987
Lake Tahoe	So. Lake Tahoe	8,544
Stockton Metropolitan	Stockton	9,650
Southern California Logistics	Victorville	13,050

Source: FAA. Note: Some of these airports have restricted traffic. Many have several runways. This chart indentifies the longest runways at the airports. Several military airports are not listed.

A Named after a Los Angeles radio programmer, Lloyd Sigmund. A Sig-Alert is defined as an unplanned event that blocks one or more lanes and lasts longer than 30 minutes.

Jobs and Income
Taxes and Expenses

The bonanza years of the late 1990s having fizzled, California has been on hold for several years waiting for the next boom.

Northern California, having overloaded on high-tech industry, suffered the most from the dotcom crash. See employment rates.

On the plus side, however, commercial and residential rents dropped sharply when the dotcoms went dotgone.

Southern California, which had its shake-out with the contraction of the defense industries in the early 1990s, seemed to be weathering the economic doldrums better than Northern California.

The saving grace has been low interest rates, which have sustained home construction. By mid-2003, the stock market was showing signs of revival, leading many to hope the worst was over.

One other big problem remains: the state budget, and the budgets of the cities, counties and school districts.

With tax revenue down, many cuts will be made over the next few years. Taxes on car registrations have been increased; more increases are probably in the works.

Who invented today's yo-yo? (Answer next page.)

California's Rank In World Economy

Rank	Countries	($ Billions)
1	**United States**	$10,171
2	Japan	4,245
3	Germany	1,874
4	United Kingdom	1,406
5	**California**	1,359
6	France	1,303
7	China (excluding Hong Kong)	1,159
8	Italy	1,091
9	Canada	677
10	Mexico	618
11	Spain	578
12	Brazil	503
13	India	478
14	Korea	422
15	Netherlands	375
16	Australia	369
17	Russian Federation	310
18	Argentina	269
19	Switzerland	247
20	Belgium	228
21	Sweden	210
22	Austria	189
23	Poland	175
24	Saudi Arabia	173
25	Norway	165

Sources: California Dept. of Finance., 2001 Gross Product
NOTE: California's rank changes from year to year but always remains in the top ten, usually fifth to eighth.

A Pedro Flores, a native of the Philippines, attended UC Berkeley, then moved to Santa Barbara. In 1928, he applied for a patent on the yo-yo ("come back" in Tagalog). Flores changed the toy by looping a string around the axle instead of tying it. The first yo-yos were carved by hand and sold to neighborhood kids. Flores later sold his company to businessman Donald Duncan.

Income — Men vs. Women

Personal Income:	Men	Women	Total
$0-4,999	2,017,000	3,882,000	5,899,000
$5,000-9,999	1,003,000	1,903,000	2,906,000
$10,000-14,999	1,301,000	1,496,000	2,797,000
$15,000-19,999	1,094,000	1,043,000	2,137,000
$20,000-24,999	1,088,000	905,000	1,993,000
$25,000-29,999	784,000	775,000	1,560,000
$30,000-34,999	780,000	699,000	1,479,000
$35,000-39,999	609,000	568,000	1,177,000
$40,000-49,999	952,000	788,000	1,740,000
$50,000-74,999	1,561,000	1,026,000	2,587,000
$75,000-99,999	869,000	312,000	1,181,000
$100,000 and up	829,000	198,000	1,027,000
Mean	**$39,300**	**$21,500**	**$30,200**

How Many Men and Women in Work Force

	In Force		Not in Force	
Ages:	Men	Women	Men	Women
16-19	510,000	429,000	590,000	553,000
20-24	948,000	885,000	266,000	364,000
25-29	1,088,000	899,000	148,000	352,000
30-34	1,167,000	974,000	73,000	372,000
35-39	1,383,000	1,093,000	78,000	430,000
40-44	1,217,000	1,048,000	139,000	316,000
45-49	1,036,000	965,000	133,000	309,000
50-54	894,000	684,000	138,000	239,000
55-59	546,000	501,000	129,000	352,000
60-64	317,000	252,000	204,000	313,000
65-69	153,000	91,000	339,000	428,000
70+	128,000	101,000	912,000	1,375,000
Total	**9,387,000**	**7,921,000**	**3,148,000**	**5,402,000**

Population Survey, 2001, California Dept. of Finance.

 What powerful California lobbyist of the 1940s destroyed his career by posing with a dummy on his knee? (Answer next page.)

Median Income by County
Ranked by Joint Tax Returns

	Joint Returns	All returns
Marin	$101,660	$46,696
Santa Clara	89,475	45,214
San Mateo	84,760	44,270
Contra Costa	79,612	42,052
Alameda	74,307	37,580
Placer	68,126	37,962
El Dorado	65,935	39,104
Sonoma	65,323	34,862
Santa Cruz	65,176	32,194
Orange	65,024	33,515
Solano	64,448	35,856
Ventura	63,998	33,412
San Benito	63,571	33,718
Napa	61,301	34,496
San Francisco	61,190	37,458
Sacramento	58,289	31,939
Yolo	58,155	29,382
San Diego	56,672	30,405
San Luis Obispo	55,009	30,163
Nevada	54,950	32,079
Santa Barbara	54,190	29,599
San Joaquin	53,625	29,664
Alpine	51,999	29,333
Monterey	51,582	28,392
Mono	51,549	26,351
Lassen	50,865	33,134
Amador	50,565	31,806
San Bernardino	50,021	28,053
Riverside	49,825	27,888
Calaveras	49,190	31,420

A Lobbyist Artie Samish, dubbed "The Secret Boss of California," in 1949 posed for a photo with a dummy, "Mr. Legislature." The uproar turned politicians against Samish, who was later sent to prison for tax evasion. Some limits were placed on lobbyists but to this day they remain a powerful force.

Median Income Rank by County (Cont.)
Ranked by Joint Tax Returns

	Joint Returns	All returns
Inyo	$49,119	$27,170
Los Angeles	48,878	26,478
Stanislaus	47,882	27,559
Plumas	47,193	29,912
Tuolumne	46,807	28,425
Kern	46,622	25,794
Humboldt	45,555	24,633
Sierra	45,537	30,105
Fresno	45,312	23,638
Mendocino	45,120	25,368
Shasta	44,822	26,590
Del Norte	44,313	25,540
Butte	43,246	24,513
Sutter	42,982	25,298
Mariposa	42,615	26,330
Kings	42,126	24,022
Madera	40,911	23,034
Lake	40,676	24,569
Merced	40,085	23,222
Tulare	38,907	21,068
Yuba	37,839	23,742
Siskiyou	37,657	23,838
Modoc	37,624	24,390
Trinity	37,208	24,083
Tehama	37,086	23,445
Glenn	36,157	22,389
Colusa	35,225	21,691
Imperial	28,550	19,094

Source: Cal. Board of Equalization 2000 Figures

Where was Lindbergh's "Spirit of St. Louis" built and by what firm? (Answer next page.)

Unemployment Rates 2003

County	Employed	Unemployed	Rate
Alameda	719,200	50,000	6.5%
Alpine	220	60	22.3%
Amador	15,770	740	4.5%
Butte	86,900	6,900	7.3%
Calaveras	15,880	1,310	7.6%
Colusa	7,540	1,320	14.9%
Contra Costa	499,100	28,500	5.4%
Del Norte	8,910	780	8.0%
El Dorado	79,000	4,500	5.3%
Fresno	348,700	53,800	13.4%
Glenn	9,150	1,260	12.1%
Humboldt	56,300	3,700	6.2%
Imperial	45,900	9,500	17.1%
Inyo	7,010	420	5.7%
Kern	268,500	35,000	11.5%
Kings	42,410	6,970	14.1%
Lake	23,670	2,250	8.7%
Lassen	10,690	680	6.0%
Los Angeles	4,426,400	299,000	6.3%
Madera	50,500	7,400	12.8%
Marin	126,500	4,700	3.6%
Mariposa	7,200	470	6.1%
Mendocino	41,020	2,960	6.7%
Merced	80,000	13,000	14.0%
Modoc	4,200	360	7.9%
Mono	5,800	410	6.6%
Monterey	186,400	16,400	8.1%
Napa	68,700	2,800	3.9%

A Charles Lindbergh was the first person to fly solo and non-stop across the Atlantic. He made the trip in 1927, taking off from New York and landing about 34 hours later in Paris. Residents of St. Louis, Missouri, put up the money to build the plane, which was constructed by Ryan Airlines of San Diego. Lindbergh's feat made him a hero and convinced many that flying was safe and practical.

Unemployment Rates 2003

County	Employed	Unemployed	Rate
Nevada	45,930	2,210	4.6%
Orange	1,504,600	56,400	3.6%
Placer	133,900	6,500	4.6%
Plumas	9,430	940	9.1%
Riverside	762,100	43,200	5.4%
Sacramento	614,400	33,300	5.1%
San Benito	24,890	2,750	10.0%
San Bernardino	822,300	48,100	5.5%
San Diego	1,419,400	60,400	4.1%
San Francisco	384,200	27,100	6.6%
San Joaquin	251,600	26,700	9.6%
San Luis Obispo	121,300	3,700	2.9%
San Mateo	356,200	18,700	5.0%
Santa Barbara	201,000	7,100	3.4%
Santa Clara	841,600	73,400	8.0%
Santa Cruz	135,200	10,400	7.1%
Shasta	75,200	5,900	7.3%
Sierra	1,200	170	12.3%
Siskiyou	16,540	1,670	9.2%
Solano	203,600	12,400	5.8%
Sonoma	253,700	12,200	4.6%
Stanislaus	192,700	25,600	11.7%
Sutter	32,500	5,400	14.2%
Tehama	24,950	1,970	7.3%
Trinity	4,930	500	9.2%
Tulare	156,400	24,500	13.5%
Tuolumne	20,920	1,440	6.5%
Ventura	400,400	19,700	4.7%
Yolo	92,300	4,600	4.7%
Yuba	18,900	3,000	13.8%

Source: State of Calif., Employment Development Dept., Labor Market Info. Div. Data for May 2003.

Who earns more? The governor of California, a U.S. Senator or a U.S. representative? (Answer next page.)

Why California is in a Fiscal Mess

Income Down (Cap. Gains, Stock Options)

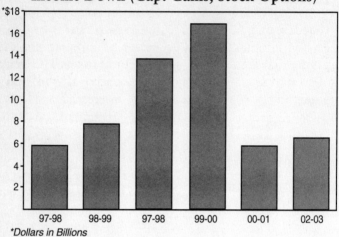

*Dollars in Billions

State Expenditures Up

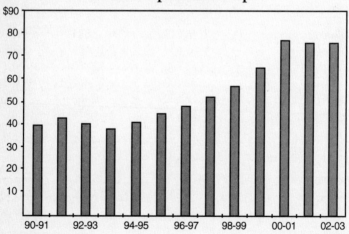

Left Column: Dollars in Billions

Source: California Legislative Analyst Office

 The governor earns the most with $175,000 annually. A U.S. senator is paid $154,700, a U.S. representative, $150,000.

Taxes: the Coming and Going

- Government spending divides into five groups: state, feds, county governments, city governments, schools and districts.

- The state government in 2002-2003 collected $94 billion in revenue. Of this, $38 billion came from personal income taxes, $26 billion sales and use taxes, $7 billion bank and corporate taxes, $7 billion motor vehicle taxes. The remaining $16 billion came mostly from tobacco, alcohol and gambling taxes, tobacco settlements, interest.

- What do state taxes buy? About 43 percent or $41 billion goes to education, 28 percent or $26 billion to health and social services, $6 billion for prisons, $6 billion for transit projects, the rest, about $15 billion, for a variety of agencies, including the Highway Patrol and state parks. The state remits a portion of the sales tax to counties and cities.

- What do our federal taxes buy? The Feds give the state government $51 billion annually. About $32 billion goes to health and welfare, $13 billion to schools and $3 billion to transit.

- What do county and city taxes buy? Cities raise money through fees. Counties levy the property tax, which in some years raises $25 billion, and use part of it for county operations and disburse the rest to schools, cities and special districts. Many city and county jobs are partially funded by state and federal monies. Counties spend their money for courts, jails, sheriff and fire protection, medical and social services; cities for police, roads, recreation, water.

- Schools and special districts. These also draw funds from the property tax. Many school districts have passed property tax increases to renovate and build facilities.

- State Bonds. Approved by voters, they are used to build schools, roads, and a variety of projects. In 2002-2003, the state spent $7 billion on bond projects.

How much do tourists spend in the state and how many people work in tourist-related businesses? (Answer next page.)

How We Are Taxed

State Taxes

- Personal Income: 1% to 9.3%

- Sales and use: 6%

- Corporation:

    General Corporation 8.8%

    Financial Corporation 10.8%

- Gasoline and Diesel Fuel: 18 cents per gallon

- Alcohol and cigarettes:

    Wine and beer 20 cents per gallon

    Sparkling wine 30 cents per gallon

    Liquor and spirits $3.30 per gallon

    Cigarette pack, 87 cents, equivalent on tobacco products

- Estate: 0.8% to 16%

- Horse racing: 0.4% to 2%

- Insurance: 2.35%

Local Taxes

- Property: 1% (plus rate to cover voter-approved debt).

- Local sales and use: 1.25% to 2.5%

- Vehicle license fee: 0.65% on price or depreciated price (recently raised but challenged in court)

- Other local: varies by jurisdiction.

Note: Simplified summaries of tax code; many exceptions.

Is California overtaxed or undertaxed? In a 1999 study, the U.S. Census Bureau reported that the average state taxed each resident $11.04 for every $100 earned. In California, the tax ran to $11.35 — slightly above the national average. New York came in at $14 — way above. Critics argue that if California wants better and more services, it should tax itself higher.

Travel and tourism pump about $76 billion a year into the California economy and employ 1,030,000. (California Division of Tourism, 2002 stats.)

8

Farm and Economy

With all its blockbuster movies rolling into theaters around the world, one might think the Hollywood rakes in more greenbacks than any other industry.

Not so, say the numbers.

In good times and bad, agriculture ranks as California's number one industry and, with sales of $28 billion, it leads all other states in agricultural sales.

Texas, bigger in land, is number two. Iowa, with its cornfields that were so attractive to Hollywood's "Field of Dreams," ranks third.

Those wanting to salute the farming efforts of other states can always do so with a glass of wine from one of California's 1,200 wineries.

California also produces 91 percent of the nation's grapes. It continues to lead the nation in every crop from almonds to walnuts and artichokes to strawberries.

Even as the number of farms in the state continues to shrink (144,000 in 1992 compared to 88,000 in 2001), productivity continues to grow.

As the state department of Food and Agriculture stated in a recent statistical review, "if it's breakfast, lunch, dinner or almost anything else, remember it was probably grown right here in California."

 Do those T.V. commercials showing happy cows in California have any basis in fact whatsoever? (Answer next page.)

Where California Leads the Nation
Crops & Commodities

Almonds
Artichokes
Apricots
Asparagus
Avocados
Beans, Black-eyed
Beans, Baby Lima
Beans, Large Lima
Beans, Garbanzo
Broccoli
Brussels Sprouts
Cabbage, Chinese
Carrots
Cauliflower
Celery
Chicory
Currants
Dates
Escarole/Endive
Figs
Flowers, Cut
Flowers, Bulbs
Flowers, Potted
Garlic
Grapes, Raisins
Grapes, Table

Grapes, Wine
Hay, Alfalfa
Hay, Small Grain
Herbs
Kale
Kiwifruit
Lemons
Lettuce, Head
Lettuce, Leaf
Lettuce, Romaine
Melons, Cantaloupe
Melons, Casaba
Melons, Honeydew
Melons, Persian
Milk, Goat
Milk
Nectarines
Nursery, Bedding
Plants
Nursery Crops
Olives
Onions
Onions, Green
Parsley
Peaches, Clingstone

Peaches, Freestone
Pears, Bartlett
Peas, Chinese
Peppers, Bell
Persimmons
Pigeons, Squabs
Pistachios
Plums
Pomegranates
Prunes
Rabbits
Rice, Sweet
Safflower
Seed, Alfalfa
Seed, Bermuda Grass
Seed, Ladino Clover
Seed, Sudan Grass
Seed, Vegetable &
Flower
Spinach
Strawberries
Tomatoes, Processing
Vegetables, Greenhouse
Vegetables, Oriental
Walnuts

Note: Boldfaced means that California is the sole producer of this item (99% plus)

If happy cows produce more milk, we have very happy cows. California cows, on the average, produce more than 2,600 gallons of milk per year, 16 percent above the national average. (Cal. Dept. of Agric.)

County Rank by Agricultural Value

Rank	County	Dollars	Rank	County	Dollars
1	Tulare	$3,493,010,000	30	San Benito	$208,718,000
2	Fresno	3,218,681,000	31	Solano	185,687,000
3	Monterey	2,746,251,000	32	Mendocino	184,124,000
4	Kern	2,254,322,000	33	San Mateo	177,109,000
5	Merced	1,703,044,000	34	Siskiyou	145,573,000
6	San Joaquin	1,389,889,000	35	Tehama	137,729,000
7	Stanislaus	1,353,300,000	36	Yuba	137,268,000
8	San Diego	1,289,708,000	37	Contra Costa	97,522,000
9	Riverside	1,124,929,000	38	Shasta	92,090,000
10	Ventura	1,053,714,000	39	Placer	75,037,000
11	Imperial	1,010,321,000	40	Lassen	58,151,000
12	Kings	951,950,000	41	Modoc	57,608,000
13	Santa Barbara	713,691,000	42	Lake	54,370,000
14	San Bernardino	703,626,000	43	Marin	50,901,000
15	Madera	651,794,000	44	El Dorado	49,209,000
16	Sonoma	589,282,000	45	Del Norte	48,596,000
17	San Luis Obispo	489,792,000	46	Plumas	47,054,000
18	Santa Cruz	365,109,000	47	Alameda	36,517,000
19	Napa	362,871,000	48	Tuolumne	32,770,000
20	Orange	319,079,000	49	Amador	27,169,000
21	Humboldt	300,299,000	50	Calaveras	26,467,000
22	Sacramento	294,979,000	51	Trinity	26,162,000
23	Santa Clara	291,048,000	52	Mariposa	22,758,000
24	Yolo	288,579,000	53	Mono	22,241,000
25	Butte	287,503,000	54	Nevada	19,030,000
26	Glenn	279,018,000	55	Inyo	16,390,000
27	Colusa	277,826,000	56	Sierra	12,640,000
28	Sutter	264,442,000	57	San Francisco	2,239,000
29	Los Angeles	258,271,000	58	Alpine	0

Q California's orange-growing industry went from seasonal to year-round thanks to what? (Answer next page.)

California's Farm Numbers & Size, 1950-2001

Year *	Number of Farms	Land in Farms (Acres)	Avg. Size of Farm (Acres)
1950	144,000	37,500	260
1955	124,000	39,000	316
1960	108,000	38,800	359
1965	82,000	37,800	461
1970	64,000	36,600	572
1975	73,000	34,300	470
1980	81,000	33,800	417
1985	79,000	32,900	416
1990	85,000	30,800	362
1991	83,000	30,500	367
1992	82,000	30,200	368
1993	85,000	29,900	352
1994	85,000	29,600	348
1995	86,000	29,300	341
1996	86,000	29,000	337
1997	87,000	28,700	330
1998	89,000	28,500	320
1999	89,000	27,800	312
2000	87,500	27,800	318
2001	88,000	27,700	315

* Until 1950, the definition of a farm was "places of 10 or more acres that had annual sales of agricultural products of $50 or more and places of less than 10 acres that had annual sales of $250 or more." Starting in 1975, the new definition of a farm is "places with annual sales of agricultural products of $1,000 or more."

Source: California Dept. of Food & Agriculture Resource Directory 2002

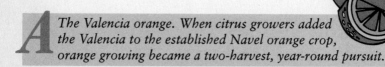

A The Valencia orange. When citrus growers added the Valencia to the established Navel orange crop, orange growing became a two-harvest, year-round pursuit.

9

Housing and Construction

Although California's economy is struggling, California homebuilders remain cautiously optimistic, thanks to low interest rates and high demand.

Industry economists predict a mixed outlook through 2004, with production climbing statewide but declining in some regions.

The dotcom bust sucked much of the vigor out of the state's economy, especially in the San Francisco Bay Area.

The Federal Reserve, however, lowered interest rates to near-record levels, prompting many move-up or first-home sales. This stabilized and boosted home prices making housing the economic star of 2003. In some areas, housing starts were up by 5 percent.

Many new homes were built in regions far removed from job centers — Tracy-Manteca-Modesto in Northern California, Riverside and San Bernardino counties and Lancaster, Palmdale, and Santa Clarita in Southern California. Traffic congestion and long commutes became even thornier issues.

Homebuilders said that even if the predictions of 180,000 new homes in 2003 are realized, California will be well below the 230,000 new homes state officials estimate are needed to meet demand.

Q Van Ness Avenue in San Francisco is an important dividing line for housing styles. Why? (Answer next page.)

Housing by County

County	Single Detached	Single Attached	Multiple 2-4 Complex	Multiple 5+ Complex	Mobile Homes
Alameda	296,683	38,786	61,286	146,732	7,650
Alpine	935	38	35	545	62
Amador	12,911	390	384	571	1,550
Butte	54,259	2,388	7,680	9,903	14,344
Calaveras	20,730	465	503	355	2,441
Colusa	5,126	229	407	389	770
Contra Costa	241,359	31,061	25,292	61,094	7,591
Del Norte	6,231	182	803	584	2,818
El Dorado	60,816	1,694	3,508	4,944	4,374
Fresno	183,871	10,059	24,403	48,195	13,346
Glenn	7,065	207	718	700	1,460
Humboldt	39,145	1,562	5,698	4,683	6,021
Imperial	26,711	1,891	3,549	6,051	7,742
Inyo	5,489	212	407	468	2,538
Kern	165,513	8,581	20,566	23,723	23,849
Kings	26,566	2,358	2,728	4,225	2,141
Lake	20,558	533	902	829	10,193
Lassen	8,470	295	513	507	2,510
Los Angeles	1,611,835	241,961	288,086	1,110,576	56,627
Madera	32,671	1,336	2,263	2,800	3,423
Marin	64,563	8,511	9,520	21,623	2,131
Mariposa	6,083	270	214	383	2,390
Mendocino	26,488	1,163	2,117	2,766	5,357
Merced	51,279	2,536	5,212	7,468	5,393
Modoc	3,318	87	97	159	1,225
Mono	4,716	1,259	2,019	3,380	972
Monterey	82,106	12,369	11,928	23,423	5,725
Napa	34,147	3,221	3,653	5,449	3,933
Nevada	38,130	871	1,674	2,188	3,621

 In the 1906 earthquake, almost all the housing east of Van Ness Avenue was lost to fire. Many of the Victorians to the west of Van Ness were saved.

Housing by County

County	Single Detached	Single Attached	Multiple 2-4 Complex	Multiple 5+ Complex	Mobile Homes
Orange	505,025	125,372	90,050	241,781	32,474
Placer	94,399	4,137	5,883	14,179	4,704
Plumas	10,646	444	375	396	2,113
Riverside	399,673	42,366	30,633	78,483	83,042
Sacramento	318,069	32,263	36,493	99,802	15,580
San Benito	13,565	1,027	1,135	885	875
San Bernardino	433,084	27,363	39,247	80,183	42,087
San Diego	554,023	98,303	79,363	298,407	47,076
San Francisco	62,952	49,355	82,055	159,095	560
San Joaquin	141,062	11,224	13,381	26,379	9,352
San Luis Obispo	70,185	6,174	8,314	11,107	11,527
San Mateo	152,070	22,719	18,385	67,709	3,537
Santa Barbara	84,998	9,765	13,472	28,792	8,567
Santa Clara	329,224	53,051	46,753	147,197	19,654
Santa Cruz	63,789	8,761	8,404	11,992	7,252
Shasta	48,607	1,457	5,499	5,307	10,813
Sierra	1,844	49	47	63	233
Siskiyou	15,807	487	1,099	1,314	3,726
Solano	100,119	6,927	10,302	19,201	4,604
Sonoma	129,895	14,044	12,032	21,708	11,366
Stanislaus	117,185	7,141	10,778	15,342	8,969
Sutter	20,966	1,186	1,908	3,780	1,694
Tehama	14,623	486	1,224	1,663	6,286
Trinity	5,355	112	106	117	2,402
Tulare	92,066	4,743	8,614	7,881	10,873
Tuolumne	22,249	652	1,172	1,074	3,889
Ventura	168,682	27,434	16,520	37,033	12,231
Yolo	36,790	4,946	4,469	15,542	3,621
Yuba	14,362	1,289	1,624	2,336	3,504

Source: Cal. Dept of Finance, Demographic Research Unit. 2003 Figures

Q What do Corona in Riverside County, Patterson in Stanislaus County and Cotati in Sonoma County have in common? (Answer next page.)

Home Prices by County
Single-Family-Detached Resales

County	Sales No.	Low	Median	High	Average
Alameda	4,331	$25,000	$415,000	$3,675,000	$455,516
Amador	138	39,500	204,000	1,095,000	230,850
Butte	848	25,000	170,000	1,759,091	190,914
Calaveras	36	73,000	250,500	850,000	285,694
Colusa	18	31,500	128,500	400,000	162,222
Contra Costa	3,943	27,000	380,000	3,400,000	461,140
El Dorado	719	25,000	290,000	3,100,000	319,421
Fresno	2,649	25,000	149,000	1,773,000	171,205
Glenn	66	25,000	127,500	285,000	127,114
Humboldt	409	31,000	176,250	535,000	187,893
Inyo	31	69,000	205,000	680,000	231,113
Kern	2,684	25,000	120,000	1,650,000	131,673
Lassen	102	34,000	127,000	479,000	143,774
Los Angeles	22,168	25,000	316,000	6,750,000	402,502
Madera	376	30,000	164,000	800,000	173,605
Marin	830	27,500	652,750	5,450,000	788,704
Mariposa	30	25,000	160,000	968,500	176,143
Mendocino	197	50,000	263,000	1,220,000	284,376
Merced	608	30,000	182,000	1,150,000	193,057
Modoc	18	32,000	73,000	225,000	96,000
Monterey	870	25,000	370,000	5,750,000	482,403
Napa	363	28,500	416,000	2,050,000	456,461
Nevada	509	25,000	310,750	6,000,000	361,802
Orange	8,377	25,000	430,000	5,400,000	511,412
Placer	1,420	30,000	300,000	3,950,000	351,539
Riverside	7,969	25,500	225,000	5,000,000	260,600
Sacramento	6,057	25,000	225,000	1,700,000	243,083
San Benito	221	100,000	375,000	1,000,000	410,100
San Bernardino	8,033	25,000	174,000	2,250,000	197,094
San Diego	8,045	25,000	375,000	8,600,000	453,521
San Francisco	966	37,000	580,000	5,525,000	705,087
San Joaquin	2,034	28,000	227,000	975,000	239,994
San Luis Obispo	906	26,500	376,500	16,025,500	430,152

 Unusual street layouts. Corona ringed its downtown with a large corona or circle. Patterson was inspired by Washington D.C. Its main streets spoke out from a hub. Cotati uses hexagon patterns in its downtown.

Home Prices by County (Cont.)

County	Sales No.	Low	Median	High	Average
San Mateo	1,793	$40,000	$587,000	$5,400,000	$679,494
Santa Barbara	692	35,000	312,000	4,625,000	422,764
Santa Clara	4,554	25,000	491,250	3,910,500	551,170
Santa Cruz	632	25,000	515,000	6,500,000	576,716
Shasta	696	25,000	157,500	700,000	172,537
Siskiyou	155	25,000	130,000	565,000	145,422
Solano	1,854	26,500	288,500	4,000,000	305,238
Sonoma	1,754	25,000	380,000	3,200,000	420,252
Stanislaus	1,634	30,000	200,000	3,975,000	213,901
Sutter	267	30,000	180,000	565,000	185,284
Tulare	1,135	25,000	114,000	585,000	126,964
Tuolumne	236	26,000	199,250	875,000	222,150
Ventura	2,825	25,000	383,000	4,800,000	425,168
Yolo	477	30,000	263,250	1,100,000	295,834
Yuba	177	25,000	140,000	450,000	157,957

Source: DataQuick Information Systems, Inc. Re-sales, April-June 2003.

Re-sales from Low-Volume Counties

County	Sales No.	Low	Median	High	Average
Alpine	7	$100,000	$178,500	$ 310,000	$200,500
Del Norte	149	25,000	98,000	530,000	122,379
Kings	411	25,000	115,000	2,500,000	146,971
Lake	220	25,000	159,250	545,000	175,850
Imperial	215	26,000	136,000	439,000	139,853
Mono	253	25,000	279,000	2,295,000	336,611
Plumas	238	25,000	120,000	920,000	154,128
Sierra	10	28,000	164,750	1,166,000	309,000
Tehama	149	40,000	136,000	559,000	154,101
Trinity	45	25,000	130,000	500,000	155,086

Source: DataQuick Information Systems, Inc. Re-sales of housing units, not necessarily single homes.
Some sales from early 2003.

 Developing a water supply helped Los Angeles County to grow but how specifically did it help the City of Los Angeles to grow? (Answer next page.)

Got California Trivia?

Got Comments?

McCormack's Guides wants to hear from you for future editions of the California Almanac.

E-mail us at bookinfo@mccormacks.com

When the towns around the City of Los Angeles wanted to secure more water, they had to annex, often begrudgingly, to the City of L.A.

10

Hollywood: The Glitz and the Glamour

Hollywood! Physically it is just a "town" in the city of Los Angeles inhabited by 210,000 shopkeepers, teachers, clerks, laborers and movie stars— with a huge emphasis on the last.

They are the ones the rest of the world comes to see, even though most of them live in other places like Beverly Hills, Bel Air or Malibu.

They fascinate us with their exploits on and off the screen — their loves, their messy divorces, their scandals. And — shades of Ronald Reagan — their political ambitions.

Their everyday lives on screen sustain a myriad of publications and paparazzi willing to depict them at their most glamorous and most unglamorous.

We queue up outside theaters, plunk down $10 bills for tickets and several more for popcorn and soda. We cozy up in stuffed chairs, suspend disbelief and watch for 90 minutes or more as curly-haired moppets dance across the screen, little girls melt wicked witches, Jedi knights race through cyberspace and Cinderella-type romances leave us searching for Kleenex. We find ourselves enchanted when we see toys take on a life of their own, see that an animated eye ball, a green troll and a persistent prehistoric squirrel, can steal our hearts and teach us valuable lessons about life. Then we sit in awe, as our super heroes like Spiderman, X-Men, and The Hulk jump from the pages of our comic books and come to life on the big screen.

Through the magic of make-believe and computer wizardry,

 In what year was the famous "HOLLYWOOD" sign built and what did it originally say? (Answer next page.)

Hollywood holds us in awe.

We know it's make-believe as we photograph ourselves outside the Bates Motel or peek into a window of what appears to be the home of the Munsters or Bewitched on the back lot tour at Universal Studios, only to find that it's just a false front of a home and the real interiors were filmed on sound stages. We also love to compare ourselves to the famous, by planting our feet in Gregory Peck's or Tom Cruise's footsteps along the Hollywood Walk of Fame or comparing handprints with those of Shirley Temple or Julia Roberts. But we keep coming back to the movies and the town that creates them. Hooray for Hollywood!

A *The towering HOLLYWOODLAND sign first appeared in 1923; the LAND part was removed in 1941.*

Best Movie/Best Director

Year	Best Movie	Best Director
1931	"Cimarron"	Norman Taurog, "Skippy"
1932	"Grand Hotel"	Frank Borzage, "Bad Girl"
1933	"Cavalcade"	Frank Lloyd, "Cavalcade"
1934	"It Happened One Night"	Frank Capra, "It Happened One Night"
1935	"Mutiny On the Bounty"	John Ford, "The Informer"
1936	"The Great Ziegfeld"	Frank Capra, "Mr. Deeds Goes to Town"
1937	"The Life of Emile Zola"	Leo McCarey, "The Awful Truth"
1938	"You Can't Take it With You"	Frank Capra, "You Can't Take it With You"
1939	"Gone With the Wind"	Victor Fleming, "Gone With the Wind"
1940	"Rebecca"	John Ford, "The Grapes of Wrath"
1941	"How Green Was My Valley"	John Ford, "How Green Was My Valley"
1942	"Mrs. Miniver"	William Wyler, "Mrs. Miniver"
1943	"Casablanca"	Michael Curtiz, "Casablanca"
1944	"Going My Way"	Leo McCarey, "Going My Way"
1945	"The Lost Weekend"	Billy Wilder, "The Lost Weekend"
1946	"The Best Years of Our Lives"	William Wyler, "The Best Years of Our Lives"
1947	"Gentleman's Agreement"	Elia Kazan, "Gentleman's Agreement"
1948	"Hamlet"	John Huston, "The Treasure of Sierra Madre"
1949	"All the Kings Men"	Joseph L. Mankiewicz, "A Letter to Three Wives"
1950	"All About Eve"	Joseph L. Mankiewicz, "All About Eve"
1951	"An American in Paris"	George Stevens, "A Place in the Sun"
1952	"The Greatest Show on Earth"	John Ford, "The Quiet Man"
1953	"From Here to Eternity"	Fred Zinnemann, "From Here to Eternity"
1954	"On the Waterfront"	Elia Kazan, "On the Waterfront"
1955	"Marty"	Delbert Mann, "Marty"
1956	"Around the World in 80 Days"	George Stevens, "Giant"
1957	"The Bridge on the River Kwai"	David Lean, "The Bridge on the River Kwai"
1958	"Gigi"	Vincente Minnelli, "Gigi"
1959	"Ben-Hur"	William Wyler, "Ben-Hur"

Q What unlikely 1960s singing star went on to become mayor of Palm Springs and a member of the U.S. House of Representatives? (Answer next page.)

Best Movie/Best Director

Year	Best Movie	Best Director
1960	"The Apartment"	Billy Wilder, "The Apartment"
1961	"West Side Story"	Robert Wise & Jerome Robbins, "West Side Story"
1962	"Lawrence of Arabia"	David Lean, "Lawrence of Arabia"
1963	"Tom Jones"	Tony Richardson, "Tom Jones"
1964	"My Fair Lady"	George Cukor, "My Fair Lady"
1965	"The Sound of Music"	Robert Wise, "The Sound of Music"
1966	"A Man for All Seasons"	Fred Zinnemann, "A Man for All Seasons"
1967	"In the Heat of the Night"	Mike Nichols, "The Graduate"
1968	"Oliver!"	Carol Reed, "Oliver!"
1969	"Midnight Cowboy"	John Schlesinger, "Midnight Cowboy"
1970	"Patton"	Franklin J. Schaffner, "Patton"
1971	"The French Connection"	William Friedkin, "The French Connection"
1972	"The Godfather"	Bob Fosse, "Cabaret"
1973	"The Sting"	George Roy Hill, "The Sting"
1974	"The Godfather Part II.	Francis Ford Coppola, "The Godfather Part II."
1975	"One Flew Over Cuckoo's Nest"	Milos Forman, "One Flew Over the Cuckoo's Nest"
1976	"Rocky"	John G. Avildsen, "Rocky"
1977	"Annie Hall"	Woody Allen, "Annie Hall"
1978	"The Deer Hunter"	Michael Cimino, "The Deer Hunter"
1979	"Kramer vs. Kramer"	Robert Benton, "Kramer vs. Kramer"
1980	"Ordinary People"	Robert Redford, "Ordinary People"
1981	"Chariots of Fire"	Warren Beatty, "Reds"
1982	"Gandhi"	Richard Attenborough, "Gandhi"
1983	"Terms of Endearment"	James L. Brooks, "Terms of Endearment"
1984	"Amadeus"	Milos Forman, "Amadeus"
1985	"Out of Africa"	Sydney Pollack, "Out of Africa"
1986	"Platoon"	Oliver Stone, "Platoon"
1987	"The Last Emperor"	Bernardo Bertolucci, "The Last Emperor"
1988	"Rain Man"	Barry Levinson, "Rain Man"

 The shorter half of the Sonny and Cher singing duo, Sonny Bono, who was killed in a skiing accident and replaced in Congress by his wife, Mary.

Best Movie/Best Director

Year	Best Movie	Best Director
1989	"Driving Miss Daisy"	Oliver Stone, "Born on the Fourth of July"
1990	"Dances with Wolves"	Kevin Costner, "Dances with Wolves"
1991	"The Silence of the Lambs"	Jonathan Demme, "The Silence of the Lambs"
1992	"Unforgiven"	Clint Eastwood, "Unforgiven"
1993	"Schindler's List"	Steven Spielberg, "Schindler's List"
1994	"Forrest Gump"	Robert Zemeckis, "Forrest Gump"
1995	"Braveheart"	Mel Gibson, "Braveheart"
1996	"The English Patient"	Anthony Minghella, "The English Patient"
1997	"Titanic"	James Cameron, "Titanic"
1998	"Shakespeare in Love"	Steven Spielberg, "Saving Private Ryan"
1999	"American Beauty"	Sam Mendes, "American Beauty"
2000	"Gladiator"	Steven Soderbergh, "Traffic"
2001	"A Beautiful Mind"	Ron Howard, "A Beautiful Mind"
2002	"Chicago"	Roman Polanski, "The Pianist"

 Every year fans of this moody 1950's movie star icon gather at the place where he was killed. Name the star and where he died. (Answer next page.)

Best Actor/Best Actress

Year	Best Actor/Movie	Best Actress/Movie
1931	Lionel Barrymore "A Free Soul"	Marie Dressler, "Min & Bill"
1932	W. Beery, "The Champ",	Helen Hayes, "The Sin of Madelon Claudet"
	F. March, "Dr. Jekyll & Mr. Hyde"	
1933	Charles Laughton, "The Private Life of Henry VIII"	Katharine Hepburn, "Morning Glory"
1934	Clark Gable, "It Happened One Night"	Claudette Colbert, "It Happened One Night"
1935	Victor McLaglen, "The Informer"	Bette Davis, "Dangerous"
1936	Paul Muni, "The Story of Louis Pasteur"	Luise Rainer, "The Great Ziegfeld"
1937	Spencer Tracy, "Captains Courageous"	Luise Rainer, "The Good Earth"
1938	Spencer Tracy, "Boys Town"	Bette Davis, "Jezebel"
1939	Robert Donat, "Goodbye Mr. Chips"	Vivien Leigh, "Gone With The Wind"
1940	James Stewart, "The Philadelphia Story"	Ginger Rogers, "Kitty Foyle"
1941	Gary Cooper, "Sergeant York"	Joan Fontaine, "Suspicion"
1942	James Cagney, "Yankee Doodle Dandy"	Greer Garson, "Mrs. Miniver"
1943	Paul Lukas, "Watch on the Rhine"	Jennifer Jones, "The Song of Bernadette"
1944	Bing Crosby, "Going My Way"	Ingrid Bergman, "Gaslight"
1945	Ray Milland, "The Lost Weekend"	Joan Crawford, "Mildred Pierce"
1946	Fredric March, "The Best Years of Our Lives"	Olivia de Havilland, "To Each His Own"
1947	Ronald Colman, "A Double Life"	Loretta Young, "The Farmer's Daughter"
1948	Laurence Olivier, "Hamlet"	Jane Wyman, "Johnny Belinda"
1949	Broderick Crawford, "All the Kings Men"	Olivia de Havilland, "The Heiress"
1950	José Ferrer, "Cyrano de Bergerac"	Judy Holliday, "Born Yesterday"
1951	Humphrey Bogart, "The African Queen"	Vivien Leigh, "A Streetcar Named Desire"
1952	Gary Cooper, "High Noon"	Shirley Booth, "Come Back, Little Sheba"
1953	William Holden, "Stalag 17"	Audrey Hepburn, "Roman Holiday"
1954	Marlon Brando, "On the Waterfront"	Grace Kelly, "The Country Girl"
1955	Ernest Borgnine, "Marty"	Anna Magnani, "The Rose Tattoo"
1956	Yul Brynner, "The King and I"	Ingrid Bergman, "Anastasia"
1957	Alec Guinness, "The Bridge on the River Kwai"	Joanne Woodward, "The Three Faces of Eve"
1958	David Niven, "Separate Tables"	Susan Hayward, "I Want To Live!"
1959	Charlton Heston, "Ben-Hur"	Simone Signoret, "Room at the Top"
1960	Burt Lancaster, "Elmer Gantry"	Elizabeth Taylor, "Butterfield 8"
1961	Maximillian Schell, "Judgment at Nuremburg"	Sophia Loren, "Two Women"

A On Sept. 30, 1955, James Dean died in a car wreck five miles north of Bakersfield, on Route 46. Dean stopped a Blackwell's Corner General Store nearby and bought a Coke and an apple, then crashed at an intersection near the base of Polonio Pass.

Best Actor/Best Actress

Year	Best Actor/Movie	Best Actress/Movie
1962	Gregory Peck, "To Kill A Mockingbird"	Anne Bancroft, "The Miracle Worker"
1963	Sidney Poitier, "Lilies of the Field"	Patricia Neal, "Hud"
1964	Rex Harrison, "My Fair Lady"	Julie Andrews, "Mary Poppins"
1965	Lee Marvin, "Cat Ballou"	Julie Christie, "Darling"
1966	Paul Scofield, "A Man for All Seasons"	Elizabeth Taylor, "Who's Afraid of Virginia Woolf?"
1967	Rod Steiger, "In the Heat of the Night"	Katharine Hepburn, "Guess Who's Coming to Dinner"
1968	Cliff Robertson, "Charly"	Katharine Hepburn, "The Lion In Winter", Barbra Streisand, "Funny Girl"
1969	John Wayne, "True Grit"	Maggie Smith, "The Prime of Miss Jean Brodie"
1970	George C. Scott, "Patton"	Glenda Jackson, "Women in Love"
1971	Gene Hackman, "The French Connection"	Jane Fonda, "Klute"
1972	Marlon Brando, "The Godfather"	Liza Minnelli, "Cabaret"
1973	Jack Lemmon, "Save the Tiger"	Glenda Jackson, "A Touch of Class"
1974	Art Carney, "Harry and Tonto"	Ellen Burstyn, "Alice Doesn't Live Here Anymore"
1975	Jack Nicholson, "One Flew Over Cuckoo's Nest"	Louise Fletcher, "One Flew Over the Cuckoo's Nest"
1976	Peter Finch, "Network"	Faye Dunaway, "Network"
1977	Richard Dreyfuss, "The Goodbye Girl"	Diane Keaton, "Annie Hall"
1978	Jon Voight, "Coming Home"	Jane Fonda, "Coming Home"
1979	Dustin Hoffman, "Kramer vs. Kramer"	Sally Field, "Norma Rae"
1980	Robert De Niro, "Raging Bull"	Sissy Spacek, "Coal Miner's Daughter"
1981	Henry Fonda, "On Golden Pond"	Katharine Hepburn, "On Golden Pond"
1982	Ben Kingsley, "Gandhi"	Meryl Streep, "Sophie's Choice"
1983	Robert Duvall, "Tender Mercies"	Shirley MacLaine, "Terms of Endearment"
1984	F. Murray Abraham, "Amadeus"	Sally Field, "Places in the Heart"
1985	William Hurt, "Kiss of the Spider Woman"	Geraldine Page, "The Trip to Bountiful"
1986	Paul Newman, "The Color of Money"	Marlee Matlin, "Children of a Lesser God"
1987	Michael Douglas, "Wall Street"	Cher, "Moonstruck"
1988	Dustin Hoffman, "Rain Man"	Jodie Foster, "The Accused"
1989	Daniel Day-Lewis, "My Left Foot"	Jessica Tandy, "Driving Miss Daisy"
1990	Jeremy Irons, "Reversal of Fortune"	Kathy Bates, "Misery"
1991	Anthony Hopkins, "The Silence of the Lambs"	Jodie Foster, "The Silence of the Lambs"
1992	Al Pacino, "Scent of a Woman"	Emma Thompson, "Howards End"
1993	Tom Hanks, "Philadelphia"	Holly Hunter, "The Piano"

Q Of Woody Allen, Woody Harrelson and Woody Guthrie, which one once caused the shut down of the Golden Gate Bridge? (Answer next page.)

Best Actor/Best Actress

Year	Best Actor/Movie	Best Actress/Movie
1994	Tom Hanks, "Forrest Gump"	Jessica Lange, "Blue Sky"
1995	Nicolas Cage, "Leaving Las Vegas"	Susan Sarandon, "Dead Man Walking"
1996	Geoffrey Rush, "Shine"	Frances McDormand, "Fargo"
1997	Jack Nicholson, "As Good As It Gets"	Helen Hunt, "As Good As It Gets"
1998	Robert Benigni, "Life is Beautiful"	Gwyneth Paltrow, "Shakespeare in Love"
1999	Kevin Spacey, "American Beauty"	Hilary Swank, "Boys Don't Cry"
2000	Russell Crowe, "Gladiator"	Julia Roberts, "Erin Brockovich"
2001	Denzel Washington, "Training Day"	Halle Berry, "Monster's Ball"
2002	Adrien Brody, "The Pianist"	Nicole Kidman, "The Hours"

Woody Harrelson, who supports use of marijuana, climbed one of the bridge's two towers to protest the outlawing of hemp in clothing. Marijuana is derived from hemp.

Best Song

Year	Best Song	Movie
1934	"The Continental"	"The Gay Divorcee"
1935	"Lullaby of Broadway"	"Gold Diggers of 1935"
1936	"The Way You Look Tonight"	"Swing Time"
1937	"Sweet Leilani"	"Waikiki Wedding"
1938	"Thanks for the Memory"	"Big Broadcast of 1938"
1939	"Over the Rainbow"	"Wizard of Oz"
1940	"When You Wish Upon A Star"	"Pinocchio"
1941	"The Last Time I Saw Paris"	"Lady Be Good"
1942	"White Christmas"	"Holiday Inn"
1943	"You'll Never Know"	"Hello, Frisco, Hello"
1944	"Swinging on a Star"	"Going My Way"
1945	"It Might As Well Be Spring"	"State Fair"
1946	"On the Atchison, Topeka, & Santa Fe"	"The Harvey Girls"
1947	"Zip-A-Dee-Doo-Dah"	"Song of the South"
1948	"Buttons & Bows"	"The Paleface"
1949	"Baby It's Cold Outside"	"Neptune's Daughter"
1950	"Mona Lisa"	"Captain Carey, USA"
1951	"In the Cool, Cool, Cool of the Evening"	"Here Comes the Groom"
1952	"High Noon (Do Not Forsake Me, Oh My Darlin')"	"High Noon"
1953	"Secret Love"	"Calamity Jane"
1954	"Three Coins in the Fountain"	"Three Coins in the Fountain"
1955	"Love is a Many Splendored Thing"	"Love is a Many Splendored Thing"
1956	"Whatever Will Be, Will Be"	"The Man Who Knew Too Much"
1957	"All The Way"	"The Joker is Wild"
1958	"Gigi"	"Gigi"
1959	"High Hopes"	"A Hole in the Head"
1960	"Never on Sunday"	"Never on Sunday"
1961	"Moon River"	"Breakfast at Tiffany's"
1962	"Days of Wine & Roses"	"Days of Wine & Roses"
1963	"Call Me Irresponsible"	"Papa's Delicate Condition"
1964	"Chim Chim Cher-ee"	"Mary Poppins"
1965	"The Shadow of Your Smile"	"The Sandpiper"
1966	"Born Free"	"Born Free"
1967	"Talk to the Animals"	"Doctor Dolittle"
1968	"The Windmills of Your Mind"	"The Thomas Crown Affair"

 What movie inspired the annual motorcycle festival at Hollister? (Answer next page.)

Best Song

Year	Best Song	Movie
1969	"Raindrops Keep Fallin' on My Head"	"Butch Cassidy & Sundance Kid"
1970	"For All We Know"	"Lovers & Other Strangers"
1971	"Theme from Shaft"	"Shaft"
1972	"The Morning After"	"The Poseidon Adventure"
1973	"The Way We Were"	"The Way We Were"
1974	"We May Never Love Like This Again"	"The Towering Inferno"
1975	"I'm Easy"	"Nashville"
1976	"Evergreen"	"A Star is Born"
1977	"You Light Up My Life"	"You Light Up My Life"
1978	"Last Dance"	"Thank God Its Friday"
1979	"It Goes Like It Goes"	"Norma Rae"
1980	"Fame"	"Fame"
1981	"Arthur's Theme" (Best That You Can Do)	"Arthur"
1982	"Up Where We Belong"	"An Officer & A Gentleman"
1983	"Flashdance...What A Feeling"	"Flashdance"
1984	"I Just Called To Say I Love You"	"The Woman in Red"
1985	"Say You, Say Me"	"White Nights"
1986	"Take My Breath Away"	"Top Gun"
1987	"(I've Had) The Time of My Life"	"Dirty Dancing"
1988	"Let the River Run"	"Working Girl"
1989	"Under the Sea"	"The Little Mermaid"
1990	"Sooner or Later (I Always Get My Man)"	"Dick Tracy"
1991	"Beauty and the Beast"	"Beauty and the Beast"
1992	"A Whole New World"	"Aladdin"
1993	"Streets of Philadelphia"	"Philadelphia"
1994	"Can You Feel the Love Tonight"	"The Lion King"
1995	"Colors of the Wind"	"Pocahontas"
1996	"You Must Love Me"	"Evita"
1997	"My Heart Will Go On"	"Titanic"
1998	"When You Believe"	"Prince of Egypt"
1999	"You'll Be In My Heart"	"Tarzan"
2000	"Things Have Changed"	"Wonder Boys"
2001	"If I Didn't Have You"	"Monsters, Inc."
2002	"Lose Yourself"	"Eight Mile"

A *"The Wild Ones," starring Marlon Brando in one of his first major roles. The movie was inspired by the takeover of Hollister by a motorcycle gang shortly after World War II.*

Best TV Shows Through the Years

Year	#1 Show	#2 Show
1949-50	The Texaco Star Theater	Toast of the Town - Ed Sullivan
1950-51	The Texaco Star Theater	Fireside Theatre
1951-52	Arthur Godfrey's Talent Scouts	The Texaco Star Theater
1952-53	I Love Lucy	Arthur Godfrey's Talent Scouts
1953-54	I Love Lucy	Dragnet
1954-55	I Love Lucy	The Jackie Gleason Show
1955-56	The $64,000 Question	I Love Lucy
1956-57	I Love Lucy	The Ed Sullivan Show
1957-58	Gunsmoke	The Danny Thomas Show
1958-59	Gunsmoke	Wagon Train
1959-60	Gunsmoke	Wagon Train
1960-61	Gunsmoke	Wagon Train
1961-62	Wagon Train	Bonanza
1962-63	The Beverly Hillbillies	Candid Camera/ Red Skelton Show*
1963-64	The Beverly Hillbillies	Bonanza
1964-65	Bonanza	Bewitched
1965-66	Bonanza	Gomer Pyle, U.S.M.C.
1966-67	Bonanza	The Red Skelton Hour
1967-68	The Andy Griffith Show	The Lucy Show
1968-69	Rowan & Martin's Laugh-in	Gomer Pyle, U.S.M.C.
1969-70	Rowan & Martin's Laugh-in	Gunsmoke
1970-71	Marcus Welby, M.D.	The Flip Wilson Show
1971-72	All in the Family	The Flip Wilson Show
1972-73	All in the Family	Sanford and Son
1973-74	All in the Family	The Waltons
1974-75	All in the Family	Sanford and Son
1975-76	All in the Family	Rich Man, Poor Man
1976-77	Happy Days	Laverne & Shirley

 The Northern California communities of San Juan Bautista, Bodega and Santa Rosa were all used as filming locations of compelling Alfred Hitchcock movies. Which Hitchcock movies were filmed at which site? (Answer next page.)

Best TV Shows Through the Years

Year	#1 Show	#2 Show
1977-78	Laverne & Shirley	Happy Days
1978-79	Laverne & Shirley	Three's Company
1979-80	60 Minutes	Three's Company
1980-81	Dallas	60 Minutes
1981-82	Dallas (9 p.m.)	Dallas (10 p.m.)
1982-83	60 Minutes	Dallas
1983-84	Dallas	Dynasty
1984-85	Dynasty	Dallas
1985-86	Cosby Show	Family Ties
1986-87	Cosby Show	Family Ties
1987-88	Cosby Show	A Different World
1988-89	Roseanne 9 p.m./Cosby Show*	Roseanne 8:30p.m/A Different World*
1989-90	Roseanne	Cosby Show
1990-91	Cheers	60 Minutes
1991-92	60 Minutes	Roseanne
1992-93	60 Minutes	Roseanne
1993-94	Home Improvement	60 Minutes
1994-95	Seinfeld	E.R.
1995-96	E.R.	Seinfeld
1996-97	E.R.	Seinfeld
1997-98	Seinfeld	E.R.
1998-99	E.R.	Friends
1999-00	Who Wants to Be a Millionaire-Tues.	Who Wants to Be a Millionaire-Thurs.
2000-01	Survivor: The Australian Outback	E.R.
2001-02	Friends	CSI: Crime Scene Investigation

* Tie

A *Mission San Juan Bautista had the bell tower from which Kim Novak "jumped" in "Vertigo." The hamlet of Bodega was the sight of many terrifying moments from "The Birds." Santa Rosa symbolized the purity of small-town life corrupted by city slicker Joseph Cotton, who met his end on a railroad track in the movie "Shadow of a Doubt."*

Best Supporting Actor Winners

Year	Actor/Movie
1936	Walter Brennan, "Come and Get It"
1937	Joseph Schildkraut, "The Life of Emile Zola"
1938	Walter Brennan, "Kentucky"
1939	Thomas Mitchell, "Stagecoach"
1940	Walter Brennan, "The Westerner"
1941	Donald Crisp, "How Green Was My Valley"
1942	Van Heflin, "Johnny Eager"
1943	Charles Coburn, "The More the Merrier"
1944	Barry Fitzgerald, "Going my Way"
1945	James Dunn, "A Tree Grows in Brooklyn"
1946	Harold Russell, "The Best Years of Our Lives"
1947	Edmund Gwenn, "Miracle on 34th Street"
1948	Walter Huston, "The Treasure of the Sierra Madre"
1949	Dean Jagger, "Twelve O' Clock High"
1950	George Sanders, "All About Eve"
1951	Karl Malden, "A Streetcar Named Desire"
1952	Anthony Quinn, "Viva Zapata!"
1953	Frank Sinatra, "From Here to Eternity"
1954	Edmond O'Brien, "The Barefoot Contessa"
1955	Jack Lemmon, "Mister Roberts"
1956	Anthony Quinn, "Lust for Life"
1957	Red Buttons, "Sayonara"
1958	Burl Ives, "The Big Country"
1959	Hugh Griffith, "Ben-Hur"
1960	Peter Ustinov, "Spartacus"
1961	George Chakiris, "West Side Story"
1962	Ed Begley, "Sweet Bird of Youth"
1963	Melvyn Douglas, "Hud"
1964	Peter Ustinov, "Topkapi"
1965	Martin Balsam, "A Thousand Clowns"
1966	Walter Mathau, "The Fortune Cookie"
1967	George Kennedy, "Cool Hand Luke"
1968	Jack Albertson, "The Subject Was Roses"
1969	Gig Young, "They Shoot Horses, Don't They?"

 One of the most famous cities in California realized its opulence after two movie stars built their famous mansion there. Name the city, the stars, and for extra credit the mansion. (Answer next page.)

Best Supporting Actor Winners

Year	Actor/Movie
1970	John Mills, "Ryan's Daughter"
1971	Ben Johnson, "The Last Picture Show"
1972	Joel Grey, "Cabaret"
1973	John Houseman, "The Paper Chase"
1974	Robert De Niro, "The Godfather, Part II"
1975	George Burns, "The Sunshine Boys"
1976	Jason Robards, "All the President's Men"
1977	Jason Robards, "Julia"
1978	Christopher Walken, "The Deer Hunter"
1979	Melvyn Douglas, "Being There"
1980	Timothy Hutton, "Ordinary People"
1981	John Gielgud, "Arthur"
1982	Louis Gossett Jr., "An Officer and a Gentleman"
1983	Jack Nicholson, "Terms of Endearment"
1984	Haing S. Ngor, "The Killing Fields"
1985	Don Ameche, "Cocoon"
1986	Michael Caine, "Hannah and Her Sisters"
1987	Sean Connery, "The Untouchables"
1988	Kevin Kline, "A Fish Called Wanda"
1989	Denzel Washington, "Glory"
1990	Joe Pesci, "Goodfellas"
1991	Jack Palance, "City Slickers"
1992	Gene Hackman, "Unforgiven"
1993	Tommy Lee Jones, "The Fugitive"
1994	Martin Landau, "Ed Wood"
1995	Kevin Spacey, "The Usual Suspects"
1996	Cuba Gooding Jr., "Jerry Maguire"
1997	Robin Williams, "Good Will Hunting"
1998	James Coburn, "Affliction"
1999	Michael Caine, "The Cider House Rules"
2000	Benicio Del Toro, "Traffic"
2001	Jim Broadbent, "Iris"
2002	Chris Cooper, "Adaptation"

A *Beverly Hills was named in 1906 after Beverly Farms, Mass.,
by a landownwer from that state. In 1919, Douglas Fairbanks
and Mary Pickford built their famed Pickfair mansion there,
and many stars followed, including Gloria Swanson, Buster
Keaton, Charlie Chaplin and John Barrymore.*

Best Supporting Actress Winners

Year	Actress/Movie
1936	Gale Sondergaard, "Anthony Adverse"
1937	Alice Brady, "In Old Chicago"
1938	Faye Bainter, "Jezebel"
1939	Hattie McDaniel, "Gone With the Wind"
1940	Jane Darwell, "The Grapes of Wrath"
1941	Mary Astor, "The Great Lie"
1942	Teresa Wright, "Mrs. Miniver"
1943	Katina Paxinou, "For Whom the Bell Tolls"
1944	Ethel Barrymore, "None but the Lonely Heart"
1945	Anne Revere, "National Velvet"
1946	Anne Baxter, "The Razor's Edge"
1947	Celeste Holm, "Gentleman's Agreement"
1948	Claire Trevor, "Key Largo"
1949	Mercedes McCambridge, "All the King's Men"
1950	Josephine Hull, "Harvey"
1951	Kim Hunter, "A Streetcar Named Desire"
1952	Gloria Grahame, "The Bad and the Beautiful"
1953	Donna Reed, "From Here to Eternity"
1954	Eva Marie Saint, "On the Waterfront"
1955	Jo Van Fleet, "East of Eden"
1956	Dorothy Malone, "Written on the Wind"
1957	Miyoshi Umeki, "Sayonara"
1958	Wendy Hiller, "Separate Tables"
1959	Shelley Winters, "The Diary of Anne Frank"
1960	Shirley Jones, "Elmer Gantry"
1961	Rita Moreno, "West Side Story"
1962	Patty Duke, "The Miracle Worker"
1963	Margaret Rutherford, "The V.I.P.s"
1964	Lila Kedrova, "Zorba the Greek"
1965	Shelley Winters, "A Patch of Blue"
1966	Sandy Dennis, "Who's Afraid of Virginia Woolf?"
1967	Estelle Parsons, "Bonnie and Clyde"
1968	Ruth Gordon, "Rosemary's Baby"
1969	Goldie Hawn, "Cactus Flower"

 A fire in what California city served as the backdrop for the "burning of Atlanta" in "Gone With the Wind"? (Answer next page.)

Best Supporting Actress Winners

Year	Actress/Movie
1970	Helen Hayes, "Airport"
1971	Cloris Leachman, "The Last Picture Show"
1972	Eileen Heckart, "Butterflies Are Free"
1973	Tatum O'Neal, "Paper Moon"
1974	Ingrid Bergman, "Murder on the Orient Express"
1975	Lee Grant, "Shampoo"
1976	Beatrice Straight, "Network"
1977	Vanessa Redgrave, "Julia"
1978	Maggie Smith, "California Suite"
1979	Meryl Streep, "Kramer vs. Kramer"
1980	Mary Steenburgen, "Melvin and Howard"
1981	Maureen Stapleton, "Reds"
1982	Jessica Lange, "Tootsie"
1983	Linda Hunt, "The Year of Living Dangerously"
1984	Peggy Ashcroft, "A Passage to India"
1985	Anjelica Huston, "Prizzi's Honor"
1986	Dianne Wiest, "Hannah and Her Sisters"
1987	Olympia Dukakis, "Moonstruck"
1988	Geena Davis, "The Accidental Tourist"
1989	Brenda Fricker, "My Left Foot"
1990	Whoopi Goldberg, "Ghost"
1991	Mercedes Ruehl, "The Fisher King"
1992	Marisa Tomei, "My Cousin Vinny"
1993	Anna Paquin, "The Piano"
1994	Dianne Wiest, "Bullets Over Broadway"
1995	Mira Sorvino, "Mighty Aphrodite"
1996	Juliette Binoche, "The English Patient"
1997	Kim Basinger, "L.A. Confidential"
1998	Judi Dench, "Shakespeare in Love"
1999	Angelina Jolie, "Girl, Interrupted"
2000	Marcia Gay Harden, "Pollock"
2001	Jennifer Connelly, "A Beautiful Mind"
2002	Catherine Zeta-Jones, "Chicago"

 Culver City. *The film crew burned down a bunch of old sets on the MGM studio backlot. The fire was so large the residents called the fire department fearing that MGM was burning down.*

California-Born Celebrities

Celebrity	Birthplace	Date of Birth
Ben Affleck	Berkeley	08/15/72
Jennifer Aniston	Sherman Oaks	02/11/69
Christina Applegate	Los Angeles	11/25/71
Tyra Banks	Inglewood	12/04/73
Drew Barrymore	Los Angeles	02/22/75
Candice Bergen	Beverly Hills	05/09/46
Benjamin Bratt	San Francisco	12/16/63
Jeff Bridges	Los Angeles	12/04/49
Nicolas Cage	Long Beach	01/07/64
Cher	El Centro	05/20/46
Kevin Costner	Lynwood	01/18/55
Ted Danson	San Diego	12/29/47
Cameron Diaz	San Diego	08/30/72
Robert Duvall	San Diego	01/05/31
Clint Eastwood	San Francisco	05/31/30
Jenna Elfman	Los Angeles	09/30/71
Mia Farrow	Los Angeles	02/09/45
Sally Field	Pasadena	11/06/46
Carrie Fisher	Burbank	10/21/56
Bridget Fonda	Los Angeles	01/27/64
Jodie Foster	Los Angeles	11/19/62
Gene Hackman	San Bernardino	01/30/30
Tom Hanks	Concord	07/09/56
Josh Hartnett	San Francisco	07/21/78
Dustin Hoffman	Los Angeles	08/08/37
Kate Hudson	Los Angeles	04/19/79
Helen Hunt	Los Angeles	06/15/63
Anjelica Huston	Los Angeles	07/08/51
Chris Isaak	Stockton	06/26/56
Angelina Jolie	Los Angeles	06/04/75
Ashley Judd	Los Angeles	04/19/68
Diane Keaton	Los Angeles	01/05/46
Val Kilmer	Los Angeles	12/31/59

 Several California-born film stars went on to become heavy hitters in the political world. Which idol was later appointed ambassador to Czechoslovakia? (Hint: Not listed above.) (Answer next page.)

California-Born Celebrities

Celebrity	Birthplace	Date of Birth
Lisa Kudrow	Encino	07/30/63
Heather Locklear	Los Angeles	09/25/61
Courtney Love	San Francisco	07/09/64
George Lucas	Modesto	05/14/44
Tobey Maguire	Santa Monica	06/27/75
Liza Minnelli	Los Angeles	03/12/46
Gwyneth Paltrow	Los Angeles	09/27/72
Sean Penn	Burbank	08/17/60
Michelle Pfeiffer	Santa Ana	04/29/58
Bonnie Raitt	Burbank	11/08/49
Robert Redford	Santa Monica	08/18/36
Christina Ricci	Santa Monica	02/12/80
Tim Robbins	West Covina	10/16/58
Rene Russo	Burbank	02/17/54
Charles Sheen	Los Angeles	09/03/65
Alicia Silverstone	San Francisco	10/04/76
Christy Turlington	Walnut Creek	01/02/69

 The "Little General," Shirley Temple, was born in Santa Monica, California.

Top Theme Parks

Top Amusement/Theme Parks

Disneyland	Anaheim	12,720,500
Universal Studios	Hollywood	5,200,000
Disney's California Adventure	Anaheim	4,700,000
SeaWorld	San Diego	4,000,000
Knott's Berry Farm	Buena Park	3,624,890
Six Flags Magic Mountain	Valencia	3,100,000
Santa Cruz Beach Boardwalk	Santa Cruz	3,000,000
Six Flags Marine World	Vallejo	1,900,000
Paramount's Great America	Santa Clara	1,820,000
Monterey Bay Aquarium	Monterey	1,719,296

Sources: "Amusement Business", Monterey Bay Aquarium, 2003. Based on 2002 visits.

Top Ten National Parks

Golden Gate National Recreation Area	13,961,300
San Francisco Maritime Museum	3,558,500
Yosemite National Park	3,468,200
Point Reyes National Seashore	2,421,500
Joshua Tree National Park	1,156,700
Cabrillo National Monument	1,130,200
Death Valley National Park	932,000
Sequoia National Park	923,400
Whiskeytown-Shasta-Trinity National Recreation Area	702,960
Channel Islands National Park	631,700

Source: National Park Service, 2003. Based on 2002 visits.

 What famous floating monument in Long Beach was used in the 1972 movie, "The Poseidon Adventure"? (Answer next page.)

Hollywood Film Locations

Ambassador Hotel, Wilshire Blvd., LA
LA Story
Forrest Gump
Sister Act
Man on the Moon
Apollo 13
That Thing You Do!

Arboretum, Arcadia
Fantasy Island
Notorious
The Best Years of Our Lives
Terminator 2

Greystone Mansion, Beverly Hills
Indecent Proposal
Batman & Robin
The Big Lebowski
Death Becomes Her
Rush Hour
Clueless
Ghostbusters
The Witches of Eastwick
X-Men
The Fabulous Baker Boys
The Bodyguard
All of Me
Nixon

Griffifth Park, Hollywood Hills
Rebel Without A Cause
The Terminator
The Rocketeer
Devil in a Blue Dress
Jurassic Park
Bowfinger

Huntington Library, San Marino
Indecent Proposal
The Wedding Singer
My Best Friend's Wedding
The Great Gatsby
The Little Princess

Malibu Creek State Park
Planet of the Apes
M*A*S*H
How Green Was My Valley
Butch Cassidy and the Sundance Kid

Union Station, Downtown LA
The Way We Were
Nick of Time
Ferris Bueller's Day Off
Bugsy
Blade Runner
The Fabulous Baker Boys
True Confessions

Venice Beach & Boardwalk
Xanadu
Falling Down
Mixed Nuts
Jerry Maguire
White Men Can't Jump

Westin Bonaventure Hotel, LA
True Lies
In the Line of Fire
Strange Days
Lethal Weapon 2
Rain Man

The Queen Mary was the actual ship used to portray the ill-fated "Poseidon" in the film.

11

Sports

Welcome to California— state of champions.

California has produced champion athletes in a multitude of sports ranging from the Olympics to the Super Bowl with many more in between.

Blame it on the climate and the terrain. There are no blizzards or sustained triple-digit heat waves to disrupt year-round outdoor training for outdoor sports. Rain rarely cancels a baseball game here. Skiers have the mountains and runners have the valleys.

Professional football and baseball teams in California always make the championship race exciting even when they are eliminated in the playoffs. Super Bowl champions include the 49ers and the Raiders.

We know, we know ... No professional football team graces Los Angeles, Orange, Riverside and San Bernardino counties, the most populous region by far in the state, but one day, we can hope, one will come.

Besides the A's, World Series champions include the Dodgers and the Angels as well as Stanford University (College World Series).

Basketball powerhouses include the Los Angeles Lakers, Sacramento Kings, UCLA and USC.

Olympic gold medallists include ice skaters Dorothy Hamill, Christy Yamaguchi and Michelle Kwan, swimmer Mark Spitz, diver Greg Louganis.

Q Joe DiMaggio learned to hit and run on the sandlots of San Francisco but he was born in what town? (Answer next page.)

California Rose Bowl Teams

1902	Stanford 0, Michigan State 49	1954	UCLA 20, Michigan St. 28
1918	Mare Island 19, Camp Lewis 17	1955	USC 7, Ohio St. 20
1919	Mare Island 0, Great Lakes 17	1956	UCLA 14, Michigan St. 17
1921	U.C. Berkeley 28, Ohio St. 0	1959	U.C. Berkeley 12, Iowa 38
1922	U.C. Berkeley 0, Wash. & Jeff.. 0	1962	UCLA 3, Minnesota 21
1923	USC 14, Penn St. 0	1963	USC 42, Wisconsin 37
1925	Stanford 10, Notre Dame 27	1966	UCLA 14, Michigan St. 12
1927	Stanford 7, Alabama 7	1967	USC 13, Purdue 14
1928	Stanford 7, Pittsburgh 6	1968	USC 14, Indiana 3
1929	U.C. Berkeley 7, Georgia Tech 8	1969	USC 16, Ohio St. 27
1930	USC 47, Pittsburgh 14	1970	USC 10, Michigan 3
1932	USC 21, Tulane 12	1971	Stanford 27, Ohio St. 17
1933	USC 35, Pittsburgh 0	1972	Stanford 13, Michigan St.12
1934	Stanford 0, Columbia 7	1973	USC 42, Ohio St. 17
1935	Stanford 13, Alabama 29	1974	USC 21, Ohio St. 42
1936	Stanford 7, SMU 0	1975	USC 18, Ohio St. 17
1938	U.C. Berkeley 13, Alabama 0	1976	UCLA 23, Ohio St. 10
1939	USC 7, Duke 3	1977	USC 14, Michigan 6
1940	USC 14, Tennessee 0	1979	USC 17, Michigan 10
1941	Stanford 21, Nebraska 13	1980	USC 17, Ohio St. 16
1943	UCLA 0, Georgia 9	1983	UCLA 24, Michigan 14
1944	USC 29, Washington 0	1984	UCLA 45, Illinois 9
1945	USC 25, Tennessee 0	1985	USC 20, Ohio St. 17
1946	USC 14, Alabama 34	1986	UCLA 45, Iowa 28
1947	UCLA 14, Illinois 45	1988	USC 17, Michigan St. 20
1948	USC 0, Michigan 49	1989	USC 14, Michigan 22
1949	U.C. Berkeley 14, Northwestern 20	1990	USC 17, Michigan 10
1950	U.C. Berkeley 14, Ohio St. 17	1994	UCLA 16, Wisconsin 21
1951	U.C. Berkeley 6, Michigan 14	1996	USC 41, Northwestern 32
1952	Stanford 7, Illinois 40	1999	UCLA 31, Wisconsin 38
1953	USC 7, Wisconsin 0	2000	Stanford 9, Wisconsin 17

DiMaggio was born in the Northern California town of Martinez.

Cy Young Award Winners
From California Teams

The following pitchers were voted best in their leagues by the Baseball Writers Association of America.

1962	Don Drysdale, Dodgers	1974 (NL)	Mike Marshall, Dodgers
1963	Sandy Koufax, Dodgers	1976 (NL)	Randy Jones, Padres
1964	Dean Chance, Angels	1978 (NL)	Gaylord Perry, Padres
1965	Sandy Koufax, Dodgers	1981 (NL)	Fernando Valenzuela, Dodgers
1966	Sandy Koufax, Dodgers	1988 (NL)	Orel Hershiser, Dodgers
1967 (NL)	Mike McCormick, Giants	1989 (NL)	Mark Davis, Padres
1971 (AL)	Vida Blue, Athletics	1990 (AL)	Bob Welch, Athletics
1974 (AL)	Catfish Hunter, Athletics	1992 (AL)	Dennis Eckersley, Athletics

Major League MVP Winners
From California Teams

The Baseball Writers Association of America named the following Most Valuable Players from California teams.

American League		National League	
1971	Vida Blue, Athletics pitcher	1962	Maury Wills, Dodgers infielder
1973	Reggie Jackson, Athletics outfielder	1963	Sandy Koufax, Dodgers pitcher
1979	Don Baylor, Angels outfielder	1965	Willie Mays, Giants outfielder
1988	Jose Canseco, Athletics outfielder	1969	Willie McCovey, Giants infielder
1990	Rickey Henderson, Athletics outfielder	1974	Steve Garvey, Dodgers infielder
1992	Dennis Eckersley, Athletics pitcher	1988	Kirk Gibson, Dodgers outfielder
1996	Ken Caminiti, Padres infielder	1989	Kevin Mitchell, Giants outfielder
2000	Jason Giambi, Athletics infielder	1992-3	Barry Bonds, Giants outfielder
2002	Miguel Tejada, Athletics infielder	2000	Jeff Kent, Giants infielder
		2001	Barry Bonds, Giants outfielder

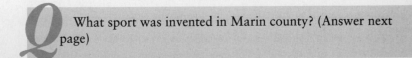

Q What sport was invented in Marin county? (Answer next page)

Heisman Trophy Winners
From California Teams

Six California players—four from USC—have won the
Heisman Trophy as college football's most valuable player of
the year, awarded by the Downtown Athletic Club of New
York.

1965 Mike Garrett, USC halfback
1967 Gary Beban, UCLA quarterback
1968 O.J. Simpson, USC halfback
1970 Jim Plunkett, Stanford quarterback
1979 Charles White, USC running back
1981 Marcus Allen, USC running back

California Super Bowl Teams

California has had more than its fair share of teams going to
the 33 Super Bowls played through 2003. Beginning with the
Oakland Raiders in Super Bowl II, here are the 12 California
contenders and how they fared.

Super Bowl II, 1968 Green Bay 33, Oakland 14
Super Bowl XI, 1977 Oakland 32, Minnesota 14
Super Bowl XIV, 1980 Pittsburgh 31, LA Rams 19
Super Bowl XV, 1981 Oakland 27, Philadelphia 10
Super Bowl XVI, 1982 San Francisco 26, Cincinnati 21
Super Bowl XVIII, 1984 LA Raiders 38, Washington 9
Super Bowl XIX, 1985 San Francisco 38, Miami 16
Super Bowl XXIII, 1989 San Francisco 20, Cincinnati 16
Super Bowl XXIV, 1990 San Francisco 55, Denver 10
Super Bowl XXIX, 1995 San Francisco 49, San Diego 26
Super Bowl XXXVIII, 2003 Tampa Bay 48, Oakland 21

*Mountain biking was invented in Mill Valley and first tested
on Mt. Tamalpais in Marin county in the early 1970s.*

California NCAA Basketball Champions

In the 65 years since national championship games have been sponsored by the National Collegiate Athletic Association, California teams have appeared 17 times, winning 15, thanks largely to UCLA, which has an amazing 11-1 record in its bids for the top berth.

1942 Stanford beat Dartmouth, 53-38
1955 USF beat La Salle, 77-63
1956 USF beat Iowa, 83-71
1959 UC Berkeley beat West Virginia, 71-70
1960 Ohio State beat UC Berkeley, 75-55
1964 UCLA beat Duke, 98-83
1965 UCLA beat Michigan, 91-80
1967 UCLA beat Dayton, 79-64
1968 UCLA beat No. Carolina, 78-55
1969 UCLA beat Purdue, 92-72
1970 UCLA beat Jacksonville, 80-69
1971 UCLA beat Villanova, 68-62
1972 UCLA beat Florida St., 81-76
1973 UCLA beat Memphis St., 87-66
1975 UCLA beat Kentucky, 92-85
1980 Louisville beat UCLA, 59-54
1995 UCLA beat Arkansas, 89-78

 What happened to change surfing from a male-only sport to one also enjoyed by women and kids? (Answer next page)

Baseball's Greatest? – Willie Mays

There have been plenty of baseball greats from California teams—Sandy Koufax, Mark McGwire, Tony Gwynn—but for sheer legend, nobody beats the "Say Hey Kid," Willie Mays.

Many put the Giants center fielder in the same lofty category as Yankee legend Joe DiMaggio. Most experts today consider him "the greatest living baseball player," and many felt that way even when DiMaggio was alive.

Willie has a strong case. Even though he was never able to lift his San Francisco teammates to a World Series championship, Mays played in 20 All-Star games, was Rookie of the Year in 1951, and helped the New York Giants win the World Series three years later, when he made his legendary catch against the Cleveland Indians' Vic Wertz.

Mays is among baseball's greatest top 10 players in runs

Wooden surfboards weighing up to 150 pounds were replaced with much lighter foam boards by Southern California surfer designers.

scored, hits, home runs and total bases; he stole more bases than Ted Williams, Hank Aaron and Joe DiMaggio combined. In fact, he led the league in stolen bases four years in a row, had the most home runs in three seasons, and was the league MVP in 1954 and again 11 years later in 1965.

Even after playing 12 seasons in damp and windy Candlestick Park, Mays ended his career with 660 home runs. Allowing for his two years in the Army and all the shoulda-been homers swallowed up by Candlestick, Mays easily could have eclipsed Babe Ruth's total of 714 dingers, and possibly even Hank Aaron's record of 755.

Giants President Peter Magowan, who grew up watching Mays play in New York, said he would "routinely" make plays "that you never saw anyone else do." Former Giants Manager Dusty Baker said Mays was a baseball genius, and "there was nothing he couldn't do." And author George Will called Mays more than just a natural—a player who stole other teams' signs and took extra practice to watch how opponents reacted in game situations.

Today Willie Mays is in his 70s, still working for the Giants. Pacific Bell Park, the Giants' home, is located at 1 Willie Mays Plaza, right next to the statue of the "Say Hey Kid," the legendary Willie Mays.

What is the largest football stadium in California? (Answer next page).

California World Series Teams

While Major League Baseball didn't move to California until the arrival of the Dodgers and Giants in 1958, our teams have made up for lost time, appearing 17 times in 44 series. The Athletics and Dodgers are tied for most wins, with four apiece.

1959	Dodgers 4	White Sox 2
1962	Yankees 4	Dodgers 2
1963	Dodgers 4	Yankees 0
1965	Dodgers 4	Yankees 3
1966	Orioles 4	Dodgers 0
1972	Athletics 4	Reds 3
1973	Athletics 4	Mets 3
1974	Athletics 4	Dodgers 1
1977	Yankees 4	Dodgers 2
1978	Yankees 4	Dodgers 2
1981	Dodgers 4	Yankees 2
1984	Tigers 4	Padres 1
1988	Dodgers 4	Athletics 1
1989	Athletics 4	Giants 0
1990	Reds 4	Athletics 0
1998	Yankees 4	Padres 0
2002	Angels 4	Giants 3

The Rosebowl in Pasadena, the fifth-largest in the U.S., holds 98,636 and was built in 1922.

12

Health and Welfare

How Are You Feeling?
When Asked, Men and Women said, I feel ...

Health	Men	Percent	Women	Percent	Total	Percent
Excellent	3,298,000	29.3	3,367,000	28.0	6,665,000	28.6
Very Good	3,523,000	31.3	3,547,000	29.5	7,070,000	30.4
Good	3,053,000	27.2	3,319,000	27.6	6,372,000	27.4
Fair	945,000	8.4	1,192,000	9.9	2,137,000	9.2
Poor	429,000	3.8	596,000	5.0	1,025,000	4.4
Total	11,249,000	100.0	12,020,000	100.0	23,269,000	100.0

Survey, 2001, California Dept. of Finance. Persons age 21 plus.

Who Has Health Insurance
Coverage by Age

Ages	Covered*	Not Covered	Total	% of Age Not Covered
0-17	8,251,000	1,507,000	9,758,000	15.4
18-34	6,224,000	2,455,000	8,679,000	28.3
35-49	6,752,000	1,445,000	8,197,000	17.6
50-64	3,757,000	817,000	4,574,000	17.9
65+	3,470,000	57,000	3,527,000	1.6
Total	28,454,000	6,281,000	34,735,000	18.1

*Persons may be covered by more than one type of health insurance.
Population Survey, 2001, California Dept. of Finance, data from 2000.

Q How much has the smoking rate gone down since California's anti-smoking campaign began in 1988? 27%, 33%, 45%, 60% (Answer next page.)

Deaths By Year Of Death, California Counties
1990-2001 (By Place Of Residence)

COUNTY	1990	1995	2001
CALIFORNIA	213,766	222,626	232,790
Alameda	9,680	9,924	9,727
Alpine	5	1	4
Amador	255	358	397
Butte	1,980	2,128	2,240
Calaveras	329	379	370
Colusa	160	150	143
Contra Costa	5,661	6,320	6,858
Del Norte	223	238	264
El Dorado	929	1,026	1,161
Fresno	4,835	5,241	5,582
Glenn	223	253	224
Humboldt	1,080	1,087	1,294
Imperial	830	798	826
Inyo	209	203	212
Kern	4,014	4,453	4,868
Kings	604	687	703
Lake	728	804	814
Lassen	181	167	204
Los Angeles	62,605	60,953	59,774
Madera	679	816	937
Marin	1,700	1,855	1,879
Mariposa	132	177	151
Mendocino	733	762	855
Merced	1,116	1,238	1,395
Modoc	114	97	101
Mono	33	25	48
Monterey	2,247	2,278	2,470
Napa	1,147	1,238	1,272
Nevada	732	780	932
Orange	14,673	15,250	16,729
Placer	1,317	1,491	1,982
Plumas	180	191	204

Thanks to more awareness of tobacco marketing ploys, the true risks of smoking and higher cigarette taxes, California's smoking rate has decreased 60% in the past 15 years.

Deaths By Year Of Death, California Counties
1990-2001 (By Place Of Residence)

COUNTY	1990	1995	2001
Riverside	9,515	11,002	12,739
Sacramento	7,663	8,467	9,373
San Benito	255	241	272
San Bernardino	9,493	10,448	11,384
San Diego	17,058	18,131	19,871
San Francisco	8,161	7,840	6,489
San Joaquin	3,813	3,914	4,465
San Luis Obispo	1,777	1,896	2,015
San Mateo	4,828	5,011	4,768
Santa Barbara	2,568	2,828	2,907
Santa Clara	8,233	8,578	8,765
Santa Cruz	1,663	1,725	1,696
Shasta	1,369	1,540	1,778
Sierra	35	28	40
Siskiyou	465	518	517
Solano	2,040	2,330	2,493
Sonoma	3,236	3,456	3,872
Stanislaus	2,715	3,171	3,577
Sutter	553	618	676
Tehama	549	626	633
Trinity	134	130	142
Tulare	2,489	2,640	2,690
Tuolumne	456	497	598
Ventura	3,969	4,100	4,729

Source: California Dept. of Health Services

How much does the tobacco industry pay to California every year to settle lawsuits:
- A. $100,000
- B. $1 million
- C. $100 million
- D. $1 billion

What Kills Us

County	Heart	Cancer	Brain	Respiratory
California	69,0045	3,8101	8,0781	3,056
Alameda	2,846	2,478	892	460
Alpine	0	0	0	1
Amador	122	83	38	15
Butte	641	498	165	142
Calaveras	101	87	34	24
Colusa	51	32	6	10
Contra Costa	1,916	1,672	588	358
Del Norte	79	50	17	16
El Dorado	324	295	66	71
Fresno	1,622	1,159	444	291
Glenn	48	49	18	12
Humboldt	328	303	72	110
Imperial	200	185	57	35
Inyo	62	52	15	20
Kern	1,552	1,067	282	335
Kings	172	149	58	43
Lake	216	190	70	72
Lassen	59	38	17	11
Los Angeles	20,983	14,528	4,550	3,223
Madera	271	200	67	47
Marin	534	453	188	105
Mariposa	45	33	12	11
Mendocino	215	208	76	57
Merced	375	300	127	87
Modoc	27	20	9	8
Mono	9	12	3	5
Monterey	645	529	225	126
Napa	325	308	128	76
Nevada	262	232	98	52
Orange	5,184	4,091	1,290	913
Placer	548	513	163	117
Plumas	52	63	15	19

California receives $1 billion per year, with $500 million going to the government and $500 million divided among the counties. (California Dept. of Health Services)

What Kills Us *(Cont.)*

County	Accidents	Flu/Pneumonia	Diabetes	Alzheimer's
California	9,274	8,167	6,457	4,897
Alameda	373	354	294	200
Alpine	0	0	0	0
Amador	16	20	7	8
Butte	95	63	48	34
Calaveras	28	7	3	5
Colusa	5	3	1	0
Contra Costa	223	197	145	145
Del Norte	28	12	1	2
El Dorado	65	38	23	33
Fresno	315	179	181	109
Glenn	22	4	7	4
Humboldt	85	37	45	27
Imperial	62	11	39	12
Inyo	8	7	3	2
Kern	283	164	139	81
Kings	62	16	42	7
Lake	42	23	19	8
Lassen	9	3	3	6
Los Angeles	2,169	2,579	1,998	981
Madera	80	17	33	18
Marin	55	82	27	24
Mariposa	7	7	3	4
Mendocino	53	26	21	9
Merced	91	37	56	23
Modoc	8	1	5	5
Mono	4	1	2	0
Monterey	137	67	63	48
Napa	40	52	30	54
Nevada	43	22	16	22
Orange	608	648	410	378
Placer	84	69	39	73
Plumas	7	7	1	1

Q How many males and how many females in California fall below the poverty level? (Answer next page.)

What Kills Us *(Cont.)*

County	Heart	Cancer	Brain	Respiratory
Riverside	4,089	2,825	999	969
Sacramento	2,611	2,204	782	572
San Benito	57	66	16	10
San Bernardino	3,317	2,547	731	765
San Diego	5,544	4,666	1,616	1,194
San Francisco	1,788	1,491	534	280
San Joaquin	1,296	980	409	288
San Luis Obispo	575	493	148	116
San Mateo	1,282	1,236	449	248
Santa Barbara	819	683	246	140
Santa Clara	2,492	2,109	728	404
Santa Cruz	485	363	123	99
Shasta	486	379	130	133
Sierra	12	9	0	1
Siskiyou	138	132	32	39
Solano	650	645	209	142
Sonoma	983	960	351	223
Stanislaus	1,167	733	262	197
Sutter	203	148	42	44
Tehama	166	155	50	51
Trinity	27	26	13	17
Tulare	816	515	210	148
Tuolumne	166	171	35	32
Ventura	1,294	1,103	400	269
Yolo	289	272	78	82
Yuba	146	118	36	37

Source: State of California, Department of Health Services, Death Records, 2001

More females, 2,471,000, fall below the poverty level than males, 2,115,000. (Census 2000)

What Kills Us

County	Accidents	Flu/Pneumonia	Diabetes	Alzheimer's
Riverside	479	366	302	289
Sacramento	353	362	246	172
San Benito	18	7	4	7
San Bernardino	461	322	402	210
San Diego	717	701	491	779
San Francisco	281	285	153	154
San Joaquin	215	116	155	72
San Luis Obispo	85	33	42	71
San Mateo	133	187	97	132
Santa Barbara	123	102	68	68
Santa Clara	324	307	240	201
Santa Cruz	68	45	40	37
Shasta	94	57	33	29
Sierra	6	1	1	1
Siskiyou	30	12	13	13
Solano	83	77	68	75
Sonoma	132	128	83	110
Stanislaus	220	124	103	69
Sutter	32	26	15	6
Tehama	24	12	18	5
Trinity	9	5	3	1
Tulare	163	98	100	19
Tuolumne	32	14	6	7
Ventura	189	138	140	95
Yolo	48	58	31	35
Yuba	25	13	17	1

Source: State of California, Department of Health Services, Death Records, 2001

 How many California residents receive Social Security?

Live Births, California Counties
1990-2001 (By Place Of Residence)

COUNTY	1990	1995	2001
CALIFORNIA	611,666	551,226	527,371
Alameda	23,285	20,941	22,029
Alpine	12	11	12
Amador	322	247	264
Butte	2,643	2,518	2,314
Calaveras	408	382	323
Colusa	277	317	358
Contra Costa	13,589	12,483	13,126
Del Norte	381	310	275
El Dorado	1,993	1,726	1,698
Fresno	15,542	15,078	14,290
Glenn	471	442	406
Humboldt	1,809	1,573	1,500
Imperial	2,799	2,637	2,597
Inyo	254	242	180
Kern	12,488	11,942	11,723
Kings	2,277	2,141	2,134
Lake	737	675	609
Lassen	350	298	243
Los Angeles	204,124	174,862	153,523
Madera	1,843	1,994	2,187
Marin	3,042	2,614	2,865
Mariposa	185	151	153
Mendocino	1,226	1,131	1,061
Merced	4,324	4,023	3,952
Modoc	141	122	63
Mono	147	136	169
Monterey	7,908	6,810	7,176
Napa	1,498	1,463	1,565
Nevada	995	833	828

Excluding SSI, the number is 2,926,000 of whom 1,268,000 are men and 1,658,000 are women. (Census 2000)

Live Births, California Counties
1990-2001 (By Place Of Residence)

COUNTY	1990	1995	2001
Orange	51,179	48,720	45,492
Placer	2,585	2,877	3,104
Plumas	182	168	147
Riverside	25,193	24,220	25,382
Sacramento	19,582	18,730	18,922
San Benito	732	796	978
San Bernardino	33,393	30,109	29,215
San Diego	50,586	45,902	43,758
San Francisco	10,125	8,592	8,233
San Joaquin	9,882	9,051	9,811
San Luis Obispo	3,030	2,652	2,436
San Mateo	10,839	9,972	10,263
Santa Barbara	6,752	5,814	5,612
Santa Clara	28,080	25,983	27,076
Santa Cruz	4,317	3,475	3,470
Shasta	2,304	2,034	1,942
Sierra	21	23	11
Siskiyou	599	492	427
Solano	6,669	5,694	5,763
Sonoma	6,113	5,442	5,706
Stanislaus	7,913	7,284	7,586
Sutter	1,219	1,160	1,213
Tehama	787	728	636
Trinity	177	123	112
Tulare	7,248	7,150	7,319
Tuolumne	566	492	439
Ventura	12,721	12,069	11,329
Yolo	2,394	2,188	2,317
Yuba	1,408	1,184	1,049

Source: State of California, Department of Health Services, Birth Records.

 What is the median age of California men and women?

Marriages and Divorces, etc.

Status	Men	Percent	Women	Percent	Total	Percent
Single	4,540,000	35	3,792,000	27.9	8,332,000	31.5
Married	6,806,000	53	6,725,000	49.5	13,531,000	51.1
Separated	245,000	2	394,000	2.9	640,000	2.4
Widowed	271,000	2	1,260,000	9.3	1,531,000	5.8
Divorced	1,025,000	8	1,424,000	10.5	2,449,000	9.3
Total	12,887,000	100	13,595,000	100.0	26,482,000	100

Population Survey 2001, California Dept. of Finance, age 15 and older.

 The median age for men is 31; for women 33. (Census 2000)